MORE PRAISE FOR
MINDS

"*Minds at Work* makes a masterful modern case to put people at the center of every organization's value chain. Beautifully written. Thoroughly researched. Refreshing to read."

—Marcia Conner
Changemaker, Impactrepeneur, and Co-Author of *The New Social Learning*

"*Minds at Work* is a definitive blueprint for anyone striving to unlock the competitive advantage of their employees in the new knowledge cconomy."

—Wayne McCulloch
Chief Customer Officer, Kony

"What is the impact of learning in our age of autonomous productivity? *Minds at Work* provides a compelling look at what managers must do to engage the creativity of their employees in way that delivers sustainable results. Authors David Grebow and Stephen Gill offer research-backed solutions that anyone who manages—as well as those who want to manage—will want to implement. Read it now because the future is not waiting."

—John Baldoni
Inc. Top 50 Leadership Expert
Executive Coach
Author, *MOXIE*

"*Minds at Works* reminds us of the most fundamental need to build an adaptive organization, an entire company built around the flexible mindset. As is often said, 'It is not the strongest that survive, but those most adaptive to change.' If this book is sitting on your desk, open it, read it, and take the lessons it offers to heart!"

—Rich Sheridan
CEO and Chief Storyteller, Menlo Innovations
Author, *Joy, Inc.*

"In *Minds at Work,* Stephen J. Gill and David Grebow set forth a guide to help organizations move from managing hands (repetitive tasks to be optimized) to managing minds that learn and grow dynamically. The leaders' role in this new workplace is to support multiple modes of data-driven push and pull learning. Stephen and David outline a new learning organization, one that is open and transparent, full of communication and collaboration, and developing a sense of autonomy, stretch, and purpose with—not for—employees."

—Megan Torrance
Founder and Chief Energy Officer, TorranceLearning

DAVID GREBOW
AND STEPHEN J. GILL

MINDS
AT
WORK

MANAGING FOR SUCCESS IN
THE KNOWLEDGE ECONOMY

"Beautifully written. Thoroughly researched. Refreshing to read."
—MARCIA CONNER, Co-Author, *The New Social Learning*

ATD Press is an internationally renowned source of insightful and practical information on talent development, workplace learning, and professional development.

ATD Press
1640 King Street
Alexandria, VA 22314 USA

Ordering information: Books published by ATD Press can be purchased by visiting ATD's website at www.td.org/books or by calling 800.628.2783 or 703.683.8100.

Library of Congress Control Number: 2017944375

ISBN-10: 1-56286-683-4
ISBN-13: 978-1-56286-683-9
e-ISBN: 978-1-56286-826-0

ATD Press Editorial Staff
Director: Kristine Luecker
Manager: Melissa Jones
Community of Practice Manager, Management: Ryan Changcoco
Developmental Editor: Jack Harlow
Senior Associate Editor: Caroline Coppel
Cover Design: Jeff Miller, Faceout Studio
Text Design: Anthony Julien and Iris Sanchez
Printed by Versa Press, East Peoria, IL

To our wives, Susan Leigh Fry and Nanette Gill,
whose love, patience, and support helped us write this book.

CONTENTS

INTRODUCTION

We began the research for this book by looking for examples of companies that said they were learning cultures, where learning was continuous and supported in every aspect of organizational life. We never found one. We found some examples of learning cultures within companies, in various departments and units, but never consistently across the whole enterprise. We eventually realized why. A company can tell the world it has a learning culture, provide lots of learning opportunities, and supply educational technology for everyone. But if management support for learning is not apparent and constantly on display by managers every day, the original culture that supported and rewarded "not learning" will hold sway over any attempt to be a culture focused on learning.

Many CEOs do not support learning, and they are not willing to invest in the development of their employees. They seem to hope that new technology will solve their problems and they won't have to deal with people. A global study from Korn Ferry in 2016 succinctly states the problem: Of the 800 top business executives surveyed, 67 percent believed that technology will drive greater value than human capital (and 64 percent believed people are a cost, not a driver of value).[1] While human capital versus technology may be in debate, some executives still continue to focus on the technology side of the business at the expense of developing people.

We realized that a culture focused on learning needs leaders and managers focused on learning. So we started to look at the critical relationship between managers and learning. Managers are expected to direct people's daily work and performance. They are not usually expected to develop employees. That's when we found ourselves exploring new, uncharted territory, in which we discovered four big surprises.

The first was realizing that there are two types of companies, and that they have very different ways of managing how their employees work and learn. We call the first a "managing hands" company, which existed during the two Industrial Revolutions, when we made things and managed hands. We call the second a "managing minds" company, developed for the new knowledge economy corporation, in which we produce work using our minds and therefore need to manage those minds.

The managing hands company was created to meet the needs of the industrial economy. These 19th- and 20th-century companies focused on what people could produce using their hands. Work changed slowly; people needed to show up to do their jobs, and the skills they learned were relatively simple and physical. Some workers, over time, could become experts in a task or procedure and were recognized as such. Management systems—and MBA programs—were developed and used to manage all those hands, using sophisticated financial tools. Training programs that were echoes of schoolrooms were developed to show employees how to make things with their hands, using tools and operating machines.

The second type of company we looked at was a result of the 21st-century knowledge economy. These companies were trying to meet the needs of the knowledge economy and focused on what people produced with their minds. The work people did changed almost every day, as globalization forced their companies to innovate faster and faster. People were suddenly able to work anywhere and anytime, and they demanded more from their employers and the workplace. The old idea of one person being the expert had disappeared. The skills needed to perform 21st-century knowledge economy jobs were not only increasingly complex, but continuously changing. Training that had been pushed at people was being quickly supplemented by learning that was pulled when and where it was needed. Companies were forced to find innovative ways to manage the minds doing the work.

The hallmark of these managing minds companies is the way they manage learning. Without trying to self-consciously be a learning culture, they simply make learning a top priority by supporting it loudly and convincingly at all levels of management, and by providing the technology needed for people to communicate, collaborate, and learn together. Yet these companies are not widely recognized or studied for managing minds, even though they are often seen as business or industry leaders.

That led us to the next surprise. Too many of the managing hands companies we looked at were an endangered species, stuck in a 20th-century time warp. Even the MBA programs that many managers learned from were outdated. There is no way to become the smartest company on the block if you continue managing hands in a world that demands managing minds. You can't solve 21st-century problems using 20th-century solutions.

Managing hands companies find themselves trying to survive in an increasingly hypercompetitive, fast-paced, and interconnected marketplace, where the only sustainable competitive advantage is the ability to learn and move faster than the competition. Corporate Darwinism proves that a company must evolve to meet the demands of new and different environments or else perish. There are more than enough examples of extinct companies that did not—or could not—change quickly enough from managing hands to managing minds to prove this point.

The third surprise arrived when we started connecting the dots representing the companies that are managing minds. We saw examples of this new type of company all over the world, from Mexico to Brazil, the Netherlands to the United Kingdom, and everywhere in the United States. These companies all shared identifiable characteristics and measurable results. They are in every industry from manufacturing to mobile communications, construction to computer processing. They range across a continuum from hardly changing traditional to slowly moving hybrid transitional to racing ahead forward-thinking aspirational. They demonstrate their commitment to managing minds from their workscape designs to their onboarding materials to the ways they share information and make decisions to, most important, the way they develop people professionally and personally. They are clearly making learning the most important, ongoing, and pervasive aspect of their organizational culture.

These companies are part of a relatively recent worldwide trend. They are talent magnets with low turnover, producing rapid growth and profits year over year. And we believe they are the future of management and learning. They represent the direction companies must take to be successful in the 21st century. And that was the biggest surprise of all.

Management Wake-Up Call

Old maps are brilliant because the great mapmakers of the 16th and 17th centuries not only captured the places that were known, but gathered as much information from as many sources as possible to try and map uncharted territory. When they reached a place in unknown maritime waters, they would add "here there be dragons" and illustrate their maps with pictures of monsters warning explorers to beware.

Once again, we are sailing into uncharted territory. It seems as if we all went to bed one night, and when we woke up the next day, everything had changed. Yet many of us are still operating as if it were yesterday. Most management practices and principles we use today were developed in the 19th and 20th century, when managers managed hands and workers learned at a different pace. Digital technology, automation, and globalization have forever changed everything.

In the 21st-century knowledge economy, employees produce knowledge and know-how, and need to continuously learn in dramatically new ways. Yet managers everywhere are employing management principles and practices as if we're still in the prior centuries. In response, companies worldwide comprise a movement to change the way they manage people to succeed in today's knowledge economy.

The greatest mapmakers of old were not the ones who made better maps of places that were known. They gleaned insights about the places yet to be explored and mapped out the uncharted territory.[2] So that's what we have attempted to do. Our focus is on what happens to all the people—managers and the people they manage—who find themselves in this unknown place where they must learn to manage minds, in a company that tells them they are now responsible for their own learning. It is what we consider the real adventure, which needs to be explored and mapped.

The new world economic order has placed companies at an inflection point in the history of managing people and the way they learn, and managers sit at the exact center of the curve. This curve has been shaped by three major and notable economic paradigm shifts in the past 300 years, each with an attendant management approach and an educational system that helped people learn how to do their jobs.

The Agricultural Economy: We Managed Backs

The first great economic era was all about land: land for wealth, land for status, land for food. We legally defined private property. Learning was hands on, and on the farm. Education was limited to a few, delivered by tutors or small private schools and colleges for the children of wealthy landowners and landed gentry.

We used our bodies and learned to harness the power of oxen and horses. At the most extreme, we enslaved or indentured people to do the backbreaking work. In the early 1800s, picking cotton was one of the most important jobs in the U.S. economy. We managed backs, and almost 90 percent of the population in the Western world worked on farms and in the fields.[3]

The 20th-Century Industrial Economy: We Managed Hands

We harnessed steam power. Electricity became universal. We mass-produced cars, clothing, food, and more on our assembly lines and in sweat shops. The machines took over the farm work and the number of farmers dropped to below 6 percent by the end of the century.[4] Even housework changed when electricity powered washing machines, transformed ice boxes into refrigerators, and replaced brooms and dust pans with vacuum cleaners.

Educational reforms reflected this change. Public education was meant for everyone, and through a series of legislative decisions, public education reached rich and poor, urban and rural, male and female. Classroom instruction emphasized preparation for careers that were more about hands than backs. Schools emphasized efficiency over individualization in hopes of educating the masses with a curriculum designed centrally by experts that stayed consistent year to year.

Managers and employees learned to do their jobs in an exact copy of the classroom setting in which they learned to learn. The workplace became the school-place. Still, change was slow, and the process of learning something often took months and even years. People were in the same place—office or factory—day after day. The predominant method of learning was classroom based and instructor led. It was highly structured training, a model developed during World War I.[5] We developed programs or courses and pushed them out to people we thought needed them. The goal was mass training for mass production, being able to perform the same task or set of tasks the same way for as long as those skills remained useful.

Frederick Winslow Taylor, one of the first management consultants, wrote *The Principles of Scientific Management* in 1911. He developed what he called the theory, which used a stopwatch to time the way hands were used at work down to the hundredth of a minute. His time-motion studies tried to emphasize the most efficient way to manage and optimize work on the assembly line. Taylor's research became the standard for managing hands for the remainder of the 20th century.[6] His approach was all about productivity and reducing the time it takes for a worker's hands to complete a task. Management science was derived from this work and evolved into the MBA degree when companies wanted a scientific approach to management.

The 21st-Century Knowledge Economy: We Manage Minds

In the late 20th century, Peter Drucker was prescient enough to create a new name for people who labored to produce information; he called them *knowledge workers*. What these knowledge workers mass produced was know-how and ideas. They spent their days fluidly moving between thinking and talking, meeting and deciding, researching and writing. Suddenly we depended no longer on backs or hands, but on brainpower. And yet how we educate and train adult workers remains the same today.

Here's a story that illustrates how these three economic paradigms have changed. In 2007, David gave a presentation to the annual gathering of chief information officers (CIOs) at Boeing in Southern California. As the top CIO was leading David into the conference room, she told him that the building they were in had an interesting history. Built on what was originally an orange grove, the building was first used as a giant manufacturing facility for producing airplanes. When the demand for planes declined, the huge building was reconfigured into floors, offices, and cubicles. The Boeing employees who worked there sat in front of their computers producing, refining, defining, revising, discussing, and communicating ideas: Ideas for new planes. Ideas for improving the production of planes. Ideas about related projects that had something to do with planes. In approximately half a century, the same piece of land had been used by workers whose manual agricultural labor produced food; then workers who did highly skilled, industrial -economy manufacturing work that produced planes; and ultimately workers who produced ideas as part of the new knowledge economy.

The Boeing story is an example of evolution through different economies. Now in the knowledge economy, Boeing employees produce ideas, work with ideas, think about ideas, and write and talk about ideas. Of course, people then have to turn those ideas into things—planes. But even those people are followed by others who had more ideas about how to market planes, sell them, teach people to fly them, and so on.

Even many of the people we still imagine as being hands-on industrial economy workers are high-tech knowledge economy employees. Miners have gone high-tech. If you go to the bottom of a coal mine, as former Labor Secretary Robert Reich did more than 20 years ago, you see miners using very complicated, modern coal-digging equipment, complete with bright LED lights, dials, meters, and finely tuned adjustments that need to be carefully monitored and operated.[7] Even what was once the most manual of jobs has become more highly skilled, requiring people to use their minds and not just their hands to produce coal.

According to McKinsey, "as many as 45 percent of the activities individuals are paid to perform can be automated by adapting currently demonstrated technologies."[8] This portends a future where people must take on a different role than they had in the industrial economy. No longer will people be needed to make, operate, fix, or move things. We will have to use our minds to produce work. It may be using technology to augment and increase what we can do, but it is becoming more and more about the production of ideas. Success in the knowledge economy is about the ability to sift through ideas and identify the ones that can be turned into profitable products and services, and do that in a way that is respectful of the environment and the diverse people who live on this planet.

Taken as a whole, these knowledge workers are the corporate brain. In a flat and digitally interconnected world where 24/7 marketplaces are open, creating a hypercompetitive environment, the corporate brain separates the winners from the losers. It is strategic to make sure that all employees can learn as much as they need of the four types of knowledge—know-what, know-why, know-how, and know-who—anytime and anyplace.[9] In this knowledge economy, the ability to learn has become the most critical differentiator. Developing that ability is at the center of it all, and managers are the key to making that happen.

The Role of Managers

When we set out to examine the role of managers in the 21st-century knowledge economy, we never ventured far from these critical questions: What keeps them up at night? What are their pain points? What's the biggest problem managers need to solve? We identified ongoing employee issues that are at the root of many corporate problems. Employees are:

- feeling disengaged
- learning on their own; not using company resources
- demanding all things be digital
- needing far more transparency than ever
- wanting collaboration and open communication
- wanting more challenging work that enables them to grow professionally and personally.

Through our research, we found that managers often have a hard time articulating what was keeping them up at night. But they know the current system of management and learning is not helping them solve these problems, compete, and succeed in this new marketplace. They are not sure what to call it, but a new model of management and learning, the one we identify as managing minds, seems to be constantly showing up and working more effectively.

The companies worldwide that are thriving are adhering to this new model of managing minds. It has proven to be more effective in many ways; these companies are better able to:

- Increase employee and customer loyalty.
- Create happier workplaces and workers.
- Reduce costly turnover.
- Drive increased profitability.
- Provide measurably improved levels of performance.
- Continuously lead a smarter, more agile workforce.
- Generate more useful ideas.

Successfully managing minds means being able to get the best from people—their talents, thoughts, creativity, willingness to cooperate and collaborate, and feelings of trust, loyalty, and empathy. And that requires winning hearts as well as managing minds. In previous economies, employees might have hated their co-workers, managers, or job, but they were still able to crank out work with their hands. Playing well in the sandbox was not a prerequisite. Try that in a company that needs employees to be continually engaged and learning, working closely with others, and constantly producing with their minds. It doesn't work.

Table I-1 compares attributes of the 20th-century industrial economy model of managing hands with the emerging 21st-century knowledge economy approach of managing minds.

Table I-1. Management in the 20th and 21st Centuries

20th-Century Industrial Economy	21st-Century Knowledge Economy
Command and control	Collaborate and communicate
Knowledge is power	Sharing knowledge is power
Siloed organization; secretive	Open organization; transparent
Workspaces	Learning spaces
Limited technology access	Unlimited technology access
Learning is pushed	Learning is pulled

A Tale of 3 Companies

Companies fall into three general groups in relation to managing minds:
- traditional companies that are still completely managing hands
- transitional companies that are moving from managing hands to managing minds
- aspirational companies that are actively managing minds.

Traditional companies are found mainly in developing countries with a strong tradition of using cheap labor to make things. Often this means producing inexpensive items using 19th-century sweat-shop approaches to managing hands. The aspirational companies are experimenting with what works when managing minds. Aspirational companies are most companies trying to change from managing hands to managing minds.

AT&T is a great example of a transitional company that started as a managing hands company (in 1885), evolved structurally, and has more recently realized it had to quickly change—or die a slow death. In the beginning, there was AT&T, and only AT&T. As a government-approved monopoly, the company's list of firsts in the telecommunications industry is unparalleled. With the first transcontinental line, rotary phone, transatlantic phone service, mobile phone, automated switchboard, and transatlantic phone cable, AT&T was an icon of a company that managed hands and built a telecommunications industry. It all ended in 1982, when the federal government broke giant "Ma Bell" apart, allowing the company to keep only the long-distance and equipment-manufacturing business.

This was the start of an intense period of technological change and competition. From that point on, AT&T tried to expand and grow, first into the business of making computers and then, in 1991, buying a cellular company as mobile phones were beginning to take off. Trying to become a one-stop shop for all things communication, AT&T even bought the number 2 cable television provider. Then in 2002, the big surprise: SBC, the second-largest regional telephone company, bought AT&T. The company, once among the biggest monopolies in the world, the greatest leader in telecommunications technology, had been beaten by a new, disruptive Internet technology that was faster and cheaper.

And this is where the transitional part of the story begins.

AT&T's new competitors included not only Verizon and Sprint, but Amazon, Netflix, and Google. Randall Stephenson, chairman and chief executive, knew he had to reinvent the company to compete. So in 2014, he asked 280,000 employees worldwide to start a retraining program. In his mind, it was an easy choice: Take classes and begin to upgrade your skills or limit your opportunities at AT&T to zero. The company knew that a large portion of the workforce needed to learn the new digital technology, and fast. In response, Stephenson rolled out a program called Vision 2020 that combined online programs and classroom-based courses to prepare employees to work with AT&T's cloud-based system, scheduled for implementation in 2020.

The change in technology is profound. It will make copper wires, phone lines, switching equipment—and much more—obsolete, along with the related work skills. AT&T employees must learn a full range of new skills relating to everything from digital networking and cloud technology to virtualization and data science. New products need to be developed, marketed, and successfully implemented.[10]

The 2020 date is only the beginning. According to Randall Stephenson, "There is a need to retool yourself, and you should not expect to stop." Employees are supposed to take as much as 10 hours per week of online learning or find themselves "obsolete" with regard to ever-changing technology. In other words, they need to become continuous learners.[11] They need to take responsibility for learning what they need to know to remain valued in the company.

Vision 2020 is a bold idea for a giant corporation that needs to change. In Stephenson's words, "If we can't do it, mark my words, [by 2020] we'll be managing decline."[12]

Some AT&T employees are fully committed, like one product manager responsible for smartphone software. With company assistance for tuition, she leaves work at 7 p.m., studies at home until midnight, and spends Saturdays and Sundays getting her master's degree in computer science. Soon after the program's start, almost half the workforce, mostly managers, signed up, with most taking online courses in web design and development, programming, app development, and data analysis.

Not everyone is looking forward to a new high-tech career at AT&T, however. Many employees who have been with the company for years are looking forward to getting a "golden handshake" and retiring early. The company estimates that the number of retirees and people who leave because they don't want to go through the coming changes will make AT&T a leaner operation, with one-third fewer workers. And, because changing from a company that needs wires fixed and ditches dug to one specializing in cloud-based software cannot happen overnight, many employees will reach retirement age while the changes are occurring and will never experience the "new AT&T."

For the employees who are looking forward to working with the new organization, the Vision 2020 program is constantly at the forefront of their work. Weekly emails are accompanied by video programs about online learning courses. There is a company website where employees transitioning from an analog company to a software-based one can find new careers and check to make sure they have the required courses, certificates, or credentials. Coursework and grades are tracked and new, related courses are recommended. Performance reviews contain the information on these courses and note whether the employee is willing to help the company succeed by continuously learning. Promotions will be based, in part, on whether the employee keeps learning.

Not many companies can make the transition from managing hands to managing minds without some pain. AT&T is an example of how technology, automation, and globalization can force even the oldest and largest of companies to pivot and try to become a company that can compete and succeed in the 21st-century knowledge economy. AT&T's transition will require the total commitment of the company— every aspect of organizational life must support and encourage learning.

The key to AT&T's success, as with all knowledge economy companies, will be whether managers can make the shift from managing hands to managing minds. Once we recognize that the problem is using an outmoded way of managing people, we must ask, "How do I evolve from the old style of management—managing hands—that no longer seems to produce the results I need, to this new approach called managing minds?"

1

WHY MANAGEMENT NEEDS TO CHANGE

As the economic paradigms change, a corporate Darwinism takes over and the companies that fail to change and evolve disappear.

In 2012, Richard Foster's research at Yale University indicated that the average life span of a company listed in the S&P 500 index of leading U.S. companies fell by more than 50 years in the last century, from 67 years in the 1920s to just 15 years. He estimated that by 2020, more than three-quarters of the S&P 500 will be companies that we have not heard of yet.[1] More recently, in 2016, Innosight, a growth strategy consulting firm, forecasted that half of S&P 500 companies will be replaced over the next 10 years.[2] The new environment is increasingly aggressive, incessantly competitive, and constantly driven by surprise innovation and technological changes, all happening at an unprecedented pace. Yet we are still trying to use 20th-century management practices and principles to coordinate and manage people in the 21st century. We need to change the way we manage people so managers can create the best environment for everyone to develop the competencies necessary to be successful in this new environment.

We have no choice. We need to stop managing hands.

None of this, we suspect, is news. What may be new is that you are, as a manager, in charge of this change. Your primary responsibility is to lead people into a 21st-century knowledge economy that supports and sustains learning over everything else. Learning is the critical differentiator in the knowledge economy. How you manage that learning is the new competitive advantage.

We describe the 21st-century corporation as an organization that is global and virtual. People all over the world will form the intersecting nodes for a constantly humming web of communication. They will be able to continuously and seamlessly communicate and collaborate. From the individual to the group, their actions will be quick, decisive, and informed, and the results relevant, smart, and proactive.

To create this corporation, how we share information must change. As Ray Gilmartin, CEO of Merck, states, the 21st-century corporation is one in which "a hierarchy of ideas replaces the hierarchy of position."[3] The previous command-and-control structure—where knowledge was power, but only a few could access it and make decisions—will be replaced with the new structure, where sharing knowledge is the real power and decisions are made by everyone focused on the job. There is no alternative future.

Examples abound of companies that were once household names that became extinct because they did not successfully shift from a static managing hands model to a more agile and dynamic managing minds approach: Compaq, E.F. Hutton, PaineWebber, Merry-Go-Round, MCI WorldCom, Eastern Air Lines, Enron, Woolworth, Pan Am, Kodak, Standard Oil, The Pullman Company, Arthur Andersen, General Foods, TWA. Of the many factors that contributed to their demise, their slowness or inability to change the way they managed people played a major role.

If you have your doubts, look at the companies that are managing minds who filled the empty spot in the marketplace. Investment firm E.F. Hutton—whose commercial catchprase was, "When E.F.

Hutton talks, people listen"—was replaced by several technology-based brokerage houses that understood that investors wanted to disintermediate from brokers and manage their own stock portfolios. The older companies were so invested in a hands-on approach to buying and selling stocks that they missed the big new idea. Individuals no longer wanted to listen. Instead, they wanted to use a faster, cheaper, and more do-it-yourself technology that provided information to help them purchase and sell stocks without brokers.

Kodak's moment happened when senior management refused to look at digital photography as a disruptive technology. They failed to heed their own engineers, who told them that instant film was an idea whose time had come and gone. Decisions in this managing hands company were top-down and final. Kodak was so invested in manufacturing film that they ignored customers who were rapidly switching to filmless cameras. The lesson is clear: Corporations must learn to listen to their customers and employees or face the consequences.

Management Practices, Old and New

"Change or die" is not just a compelling hook to capture the imagination. It is the reality that corporations face whether they want to admit it or not. Fortunately, examples of success are everywhere. The new style of managing minds is the antidote to the problems created by trying to force-fit the 20th-century analog model into the 21st-century digital reality.

Hands are replaceable, literally: Human hands are being replaced by robotic hands every day. And managing robots is no longer a job that requires hands-on managers. This trend toward automation will not stop while technology keeps getting better and more sophisticated. One study from Oxford University found that "advanced robots are gaining enhanced senses and dexterity, allowing them to perform a broader scope of manual tasks. This is likely to change the nature of work across industries and occupations."[4] Astonishingly, robot hands can now thread a needle.

If you think threading a needle is not that big a deal, here is another example. In a kitchen in Silicon Valley, the team at Zume Pizza is hard at work. Pepe and Giorgio squirt on the sauce, and Marta spreads it in concentric circles, just like they do in Italy. Then Bruno puts the pizza in the oven to bake to perfection. And they do not even stop for a moment to catch their breaths. That's because Pepe, Giorgio, Marta, and Bruno are robots. And while human employees still apply the toppings according to the customer's wishes, it's only a matter of time before they cede that role, too. Made-to-order, ready-to-go, fully automated pizza in as little as seven minutes: As the owners are proud of saying, it's "artisanal robotic pizza."[5]

You need only to read any recent news report to see this story repeated hundreds of times:

- Foxconn has replaced 60,000 factory workers with robots.[6]
- Wendy's is replacing its lowest-paid workers with robots.[7]
- Tesla Gigafactory is using robots to build machines at its battery factory.[8]

We once used machines to build things, and we managed hands. Now we build machines to build machines. When there are no hands left, what still needs to be managed?

Minds. It's time we begin to consciously manage minds—the minds of the people who design, program, install, service, and upgrade those robotic hands, for example. Their work is the product of their thinking, creativity, and problem solving.

But where can managers learn to empower and nurture minds? We looked at the curriculums of more than 30 MBA programs and found that they are still focused on the principles and practices developed in the 20th-century industrial economy. Managers are taught about finance, big data, investment, global management, economics, strategy, executive leadership, macroeconomics, statistics, marketing, legal studies, and persuasive speaking. Harvard University has a course titled Managing Human Capital that is a discussion-based class looking at how to manage people. Modules include "Hiring and Onboarding," "Evaluating Performance," and "Talent Management," all from the perspective of traditional companies.

Management science was derived from empirical observation of workplaces designed to produce things. The MBA programs that were developed during that period could only see organizations that were managing hands as their models. It's like the scientists that thought the Earth was flat and based their research on that premise. These MBA programs emphasize what leaders need to do operationally to maximize profit in their companies. Unfortunately, this is not what is needed today. Recruiters, according to a study by Jeff Kavanaugh, are looking for "professionalism, critical thinking, teamwork, and communication."[9]

Managers need to take on new roles and responsibilities very different from the ones they are used to, have been mentored and trained to do, or have been taught to follow from their management courses or MBA programs. According to Deloitte University Press, "Ninety percent of companies are redesigning their organizations to be more dynamic, team-centric, and connected."[10] Many of these companies are trying a variety of approaches and ideas to reinvent themselves to meet the challenges they experience every day. They are getting parts of the puzzle correct, but when we looked at the companies that are managing minds, we realized they have figured out the central idea that pulls all the pieces together into a coherent picture.

The lessons are starting to be learned in some MBA programs. For example, Stanford University's Graduate School of Business teaches about managing minds in one of its courses, Redesigning Work for 21st-Century Men and Women, which tries to "explore the gap between how our organizations are designed, and what a new generation of workers desire in terms of work." It has another course called Interpersonal Dynamics. Taught since 1968, the course is currently the most popular elective. Often referred to as the "touchy feely" course, it covers many of the interpersonal issues related to communication and feedback skills.[11]

Still, the goal of Stanford's program is to make students better leaders, not managers of 21st-century companies that must manage minds to survive and thrive. In the future, we could imagine a curriculum that included courses on how to run a managing minds business, such as Characteristics of the 20th-Century Industrial Economy Organization, Moving Away From Command-and-Control Management Styles, A Focus on Learning, The Technology-Driven Workforce, Learning to Support Collaboration, Open Communication Styles, Shared Strategic Decisions, and Management Styles for the 21st-Century Knowledge Economy.

The lack of forward-looking courses is disappointing. The universities and colleges offering these programs do no one a service: not the soon-to-be managers or executives, not the people they'll manage, and certainly not the organizations that will hire them. We need to change the way we manage people, or continue to be unprepared and unable to cope with the rapid and dramatic changes occurring now. It's part of the corporate Darwinian evolution. If we start to dig, there's no shortage of corporate bones to examine.

The $92 Billion Question

Arie de Geus, former head of the strategic planning group at Royal Dutch Shell, said that "the ability to learn faster than competitors may be the only sustainable competitive advantage."[12] Companies devote most of their learning resources—money, time, effort—to formal training, yet this method of learning contributes little to overall success. Workers learn little from training programs, no matter how well designed and delivered. And those programs do little to help people learn faster than the competition.

Think about it. Arie de Geus was not talking about the kind of learning that is canned and available to everyone. The idea of learning as a competitive advantage is really about the ability to see patterns and trends, make creative leaps, take risks and learn from failures, listen to what customers are saying, and take their words to heart. It's about real learning, the kind that needs to be identified, nurtured, practiced, and constantly improved. The kind produced when managers are consciously managing with real learning as the outcome.

HR, training departments, and chief learning officers have been designing and delivering training events for more than 100 years. They have become quite good at doing this. But the future of learning in organizations is not about developing and delivering high-quality training events. It is about managing minds and the attendant learning that contributes in a measurable way to the success of the organization, regardless of how that learning occurs. The problem with canned or highly structured training programs is that people forget what they have learned before it is applied in the workplace, and training's potential positive impact is lost due to a host of organizational factors beyond the control of learning professionals.

Instructor-led programs continue to be the primary method of training; almost 49 percent of the training hours in 2015 were instructor-led.[13] Although classroom-based training has declined over the past few years and some instructor-led training is done electronically, the predominant method is still sage on the stage. Only 15 to 20 percent of participants in these programs will end up applying what they learned to achieving the strategic goals of their organizations.[14] It adds up to an incredible waste of resources. Consider that $164.2 billion was spent on learning and development activities in 2012.[15] This means that $92 billion of that was wasted.[16]

The $92 billion question is, "Why is there so little impact from formal training in organizations?" Our experience has led us to believe there are five primary reasons for the failure of traditional, instructor-led training:

1. **Timeliness.** Training, to be effective, must be delivered as close in time as possible to when it is most needed. Training programs scheduled at a specific time in the future cannot be timely. They constitute "just-in-case" training: knowledge you might need someday. Younger employees expect the knowledge and know-how they need to be available when and where they need it, anytime and anyplace. If they want training at all, they want it to be "just-in-time."

2. **Knowledge transfer.** Instructors cannot ensure that knowledge transfer occurs. Even if learning occurs during the course, there is no guarantee that it will be retained or applied on the job. In all the years during which training was seen as the answer to a corporate problem, there has been no consistent measurement of the transfer and effectiveness of training on the job. Training has been treated as the magic wand, but like all magic tricks, the problem still exists; it is just temporarily hidden.

7

3. **Increased speed of change.** Today's highly complex organizations, with their shifting customer demands and competitive pressures, have rapidly changing learning needs that require agile learners and solutions. Globalization and digital technology create new, instantaneous corporate challenges. Training that takes weeks or months to design and redesign using standard instructional methods can never keep up with new technology and new applications of that technology. No one is sure training truly worked even before the advent of these tectonic changes in the corporate landscape. We know that it does not work today.

4. **Context.** Because these programs are removed from the day-to-day activities of the workplace, they lack relevancy. The point is that when you train people to perform a job, if that training is done away from where they work, either in terms of actual space or time, they are unlikely to take the lessons back to work and use them to improve performance. Another way to look at it is that training is useful to stimulate short-term memory, but has never been proven to engage long-term memory. Simulations can work in the short term. Replicating the workplace in a lab or assessment center can work in the short term. Everything else fails to do the job and produce the desired results of improved performance over time.

5. **Sage on the stage.** The instructor-led training (ILT) method that permeates some if not all of these programs is a poor way to facilitate learning. It limits the amount and types of interaction, tends to avoid experimentation and discovery, and limits learning to the time and place of the event. If testing your short-term memory and gathering smile sheets at the end of the course is what you want to spend time and money on, keep doing instructor-led training. ILT is not worth it if what you really want are measurable results that show improved performance in the workplace and impact on the organization.

Clark Quinn summed up the situation when he wrote, "The waste of organizational resources, and learner time, is tragic. Seldom has so much been done, for so many, for so little gain."[17] This observation applies to all formal learning solutions, such as workshops, courses, seminars, online instruction, off-site events, and conferences. In the current economic environment, in which resources are becoming more limited, this is a recipe for failure. Corporations today cannot afford to waste resources. Maybe there was a time when learning events (especially off-site events) were considered perks and it did not matter how much participants learned. Those days are over.

The waste is more the result of mismanagement of expectations than poor design. Organizations do things that disable the transfer of knowledge and prevent the lessons from being applied to achieve business goals. For example, people are sent to business acumen simulations without knowing how what they learn will fit into their professional or personal growth, how they will be expected to apply what they learn to improve work performance, and what difference it will make for the organization.

ILT grew out of a managing hands approach to learning. We must shift the focus from the delivery of formal training programs to the real learning that contributes to organizational success. The answer to every problem isn't training. It's to stop managing hands and using training as the cure-all, and begin managing minds, with learning as the goal.

Many studies and experts tell us that training must focus on improving performance. However, performance improvement has always been a nebulous or difficult goal to achieve through training programs. It all starts with training programs not being high on the list of the ways learners want or need to obtain the knowledge they need to improve work. Training separates learners from one another and from the context in which they will need to adopt and adapt what they learn. We have rarely seen training alone produce a measurable return on investment, or provide a sustainable, demonstrable improvement in performance. What companies have gotten wrong is a blind and unwavering emphasis on training to solve problems and improve performance.

Rather, they should be creating connections. The greatest source of learning is from the connections people make within their organizations.

When you are managing minds, you are intentional about helping everyone make connections—with other learners, mentors and coaches, other departments, suppliers and business partners, communities of practice, and external resources.

Managers who still have one foot in the industrial economy may be dipping a toe into the knowledge economy out of a feeling of anxiety about competing in the future. These managers will not be successful given the tremendous, rapid change in our society. They must realize that they can't depend on training to prepare workers for the new world in which we live. They have to step out of the managing hands world and jump quickly with both feet into managing minds.

2

THE BENEFITS OF MANAGING MINDS

The future of how we learn in our organizations is a popular topic. But unless you are responsible for developing, delivering, managing, and measuring training and learning, keeping up with the latest learning technologies can be overwhelming. It's also irrelevant to the discussion of managing minds.

The training and learning technology discussions miss the point. Unless a company is making a basic change in the way it manages people, the tools will never have an impact on the way people think, act, and grow every day, and they won't boost performance or drive business results. A company managing hands can buy and use every tool in the training and learning toolbox, but if the use is not mandated or pushed by the organization, if sharing knowledge is not a basic tenet for working, if the knowledge isn't available anytime and anywhere, if collaboration and communication are absent, if there is no feedback, then the new tools and technologies will not make the company any smarter.

Our approach is to suggest new ways of facilitating learning that fit into managing minds. All L&D tools and technology can be utilized in this context. The three keys to successfully managing minds are essentially the competencies needed to move forward and succeed in the knowledge economy.

1. **Learning independently.** In a company that manages minds, people need to take responsibility for learning what they need to know and do. This means that they need to be aware of what they're doing now and what they may be called upon to do in the future. They need to know what is relevant for them to learn and be empowered to learn what is necessary today and in preparation for tomorrow. They need to understand that what they learn will help the company meet its business goals. They must be able to develop and maintain their own learning plans and portfolios, and be prepared to act as teachers and mentors for other people in the company. Independent learners are capable of successfully meeting the requirements of learning projects they choose, whether it's completion and a passing grade, measures of competency, or an actual project deliverable.

2. **Learning interactively.** Technology is and will continue to be an integral part of managing; people need to use the tools available today, and look for and be willing to adopt any tools developed in the future. This includes knowing the most efficient and effective way to use the technology to communicate and collaborate, as well as being confident enough to interact with the technology in ways that actively provide input to help others learn. For example, smartphones can provide workers with just-in-time information to solve a problem, operate a machine, or collaborate more effectively with an employee.

3. **Learning socially.** Being part of the collective group, acting as a dynamic node in an interconnected web of people learning continuously, is also important. To be a successful social learner means being able to empathize and relate to others, communicate effectively, collaborate cooperatively, resolve conflicts, and balance different perspectives and

opinions. Much of learning in organizations is social; therefore, it makes sense to be intentional about creating opportunities for people to connect.

These three competencies are how people learn in a company that is successfully managing minds. They differ dramatically from the ways people learned when they were in organizations that managed hands (Table 2-1).

Table 2-1. Differences Between Managing Hands and Minds

Managing Hands	Managing Minds
Passive	Active
Dependent	Independent
Fearful	Fearless
Obeying	Challenging
Closed-Minded	Open-Minded
Rigid roles	Fluid roles
Conforming	Nonconforming
Not curious	Curious
Thoughtless	Thoughtful
Unmotivated	Motivated
Following	Leading
Stupid	Smart

This last distinction is not unsupported. André Spicer, professor of organizational behavior at the Cass Business School at City, University of London, has spent years talking with hundreds of the best and brightest minds to graduate from some of the most prestigious universities. The eye-opening discovery in his 2017 book, *The Stupidity Paradox: The Power and Pitfalls of Functional Stupidity*, co-authored with Mats Alvesson, was that when people with impressive educational credentials go to work for the most well-known companies in the world, they are asked to turn off their brains. Many of the companies surveyed in the book should be managing minds.[1]

Yet the predominant environment supports—promotes, even— the traits listed on the left side of the list. This is perhaps a result of short-term thinking, in which following the rules, adding regulations without reason, not asking for justification for decisions (especially from self-appointed leaders), not asking questions, and essentially, not thinking for yourself. These managing hands traits can be found in an organization that is obedient, nice, agreeable, harmonious, and seemingly successful in the short term. The problem is the long term. Asking people not to use their minds is simply asking them to ignore personal growth and satisfaction; not pay attention to long-term organizational competitiveness, innovation, and success; and not participate in the improvement and development of society.

A recent experience proved how dangerous adhering to the old management and learning model can be. In consulting with one of the world's best-known nongovernment organizations (NGOs), David conducted an exhaustive series of interviews with managers and directors at different levels, located in countries around the globe. This NGO is funded to do work throughout the world improving health—which also means working to eradicate deadly diseases or control outbreaks. The interviews quickly revealed that members of the NGO in one country were not sharing information that could be extremely beneficial to co-workers in other countries, even though doing so could have helped eliminate suffering and save lives.

Deeper investigation revealed that the NGO had an established culture of "hoarding" learning and training, and doling it out to those that top management had decided to bring into the fold. When a favored few rose to the top in their own country, they were invited to the world headquarters, located in a vibrant, wealthy city, where they were wined, dined, and welcomed into the elite inner circle. They then moved to the headquarters city to take their new positions, where they communicated information to the other elites, occasionally returning to their home countries. There was little desire to change how the NGO managed its selected high potentials—even though changing to an organization that managed the minds of all employees could clearly make it much more agile, effective, and successful in meeting its stated goals.

This example exposes one of the dangers of managing hands. If the underlying culture is still embedded in the old command-and-control hierarchy, then selectively sharing knowledge will become another route to power. In a true managing minds organization, people instinctively believe that sharing knowledge is empowering and automatically act on that belief. This is yet one more reason to build a real managing minds organization and not just erect a facade that might pass for one.

The Corporate Brain

One way to think about the overall capability of your company is the metaphor of the Corporate IQ, which represents the total brain power of your organization. It's the collection of each employee's:

- abilities
- hard and soft skills
- capacity to learn new skills
- communication and collaboration expertise
- insight
- foresight and hindsight strength
- decision-making experience
- ability to tolerate and learn from risk
- creativity
- innovation capability.

The Corporate IQ is a way to gauge the potential and kinetic energy of your company. As mapmakers, we see the Corporate IQ as the latitude and longitude for navigating the uncharted waters of tomorrow.

Examining your Corporate IQ is a way to get a handle on how well you are managing minds, and on what chance you have to succeed. It shows you how smart your organization is today, how well it will perform tomorrow, how the expected will be handled and, most important, how the unexpected will be encountered. If your Corporate IQ is growing, you're on the right track for the future. If it's shrinking, you have a problem.

A shrinking Corporate IQ is a function of many forces at work in our digital, globalized economy:

- **Minds are not learning how to learn.** Technology has changed the learning equation. It used to be that the person who had the knowledge would control how that knowledge was shared with others. Knowledge was power. But in a managing minds environment, *sharing* knowledge is power. If people cannot learn from one another and use technology that helps them collaborate and communicate, they will not maximize their talents. Developing talent means developing the ability to learn how to learn in a high-tech world—that is, learning how individuals, teams, and the organization can acquire and apply the knowledge and skills they need to be successful. If managers were managing minds, people would be learning how to learn.

- **Minds are jumping out of the workforce.** Important company knowledge is walking out the door so quickly that the door never gets a chance to close. NPR reporter Yuki Noguchi found that, "In the U.S., roughly 10,000 people reach retirement age every day. And though not everyone who turns 65 retires right away, enough do that some companies are trying to head off the problem. . . . Losing veteran workers is a challenge."[2] When all the smart, experienced people leave, the Corporate IQ starts to shrink. Managing minds is an important part of the equation to keep talent in the company as long as possible, bring new talent up-to-speed quickly, and transfer knowledge as effectively and efficiently as possible.

- **Minds are not taking advantage of the Internet.** Today, a single individual has the collective brainpower of the Internet, and all the people connected to it. Smart people are no longer simply hired and kept inside your corporate walls. They can be found anytime, anywhere, by any one of the billions of people with a mobile device. Technology can provide managers who are ready to manage minds with an invaluable competitive advantage: people who can collaborate and communicate anytime and anywhere. Companies that don't take advantage of this collective brainpower are limiting their IQ.

- **Minds are not smart enough to beat the competition.** Smart people are everywhere, and they are finding one another and creating virtual organizations that pump out services and products at an amazing rate. Your competition may not yet have a brand or an office, but if they have access to the Internet, they can become a competitor overnight. They have easy access to all the information and support they need to bring a new product or service to market quickly and cheaply. If you don't enable everyone to be as smart as possible, you risk losing out to your smarter competition.

- **Minds are not fully engaged and not effective.** People who are bored, tired, overworked, not challenged, and disengaged are underperforming. About a third of U.S. employees find their work engaging, which hasn't changed much over the past few years.[3] This means that two-thirds are probably not learning what their company needs them to learn. Their hands may be busy, but their minds are not committed to results. They may be getting things done, but they are not contributing new ideas about better ways to do them. If they are not motivated to do their best and give their all, they are not motivated to acquire the knowledge and skills they need to be successful. As a result, the Corporate IQ will not grow, and the organization will not get smarter. Companies need to focus on the relationship between empowering people and improving employee engagement, satisfaction, and performance.

To grow their Corporate IQ, 21st-century companies must focus on managing minds and enabling learning. They must have managers and executives who model and communicate the importance of the principles that support managing minds to everyone in the company. They need an environment that facilitates and supports learning on a continuous basis because, as Darren Childs, CEO of UKTV, the United Kingdom's biggest multichannel broadcasting company, puts it, "Quick fixes and perfect workplaces are pipedreams. Crafting the perfect culture is a never-ending process. Here, nothing is set in stone. What works well now might not work in the future. We continuously experiment, learn and adapt."[4]

Companies need managers who help their direct reports learn, develop, and grow as people, and reward them for being self-managing learners. Companies must enable people to use technology to find the information they need, when and where they need it. Twenty-first-century companies need people who believe that sharing knowledge is power.

By creating and sustaining a company that is focused on learning, you can control the direction in which your company's Corporate IQ is moving. Being obsessive about managing minds will make you and your company smarter. And smarter means more successful in today's marketplace.

Managing minds is critical to ensuring that your company does not lose out because of the "brain drain." You will:

- Avoid wasting time, money, and energy on programs that don't improve performance.
- Take advantage of the technology that makes corporate brains smarter.
- Optimize the collective brainpower of the organization.
- Discover ways to engage, energize, and challenge yourself and the people with whom you work.
- Create an organization that is creative, innovative, and competitive.

Companies that are successfully managing minds share several observable characteristics:

- Senior management supports the managing minds approach.
- C-suite executives understand the business value of a continuous learning strategy.
- A learning strategy is in place and understood throughout the enterprise; it is aligned with business goals.
- Learning objectives are directly linked to corporate performance.
- Budgets are reviewed and developed at the C-suite level, with enough funding to support the learning strategy.
- A chief learning officer (CLO) is responsible for the strategy and budget for learning.
- A centralized learning function supports managers in their daily operations worldwide.

- Learning is technology enabled and continuous throughout the company.
- There is a collaborative culture that makes learning central to all activities.

The results achieved by these companies consistently help them to be the smartest, fastest-growing companies, with enviable financial results: a steady, long-term increase in revenues and value; key performance indicators moving in a positive direction; lower-than-average turnover; and greater innovation in response to competition.

Barriers to a New Approach

What gets in the way of managing minds in the workplace? What are the key barriers faced by managers? Let's look at mindset, need for control, and the work-learning dichotomy. These are the three biggest barriers.

Mindset

In a company managing minds, learning is everyone's main job. And the most important factor in learning is a person's belief system. A managing minds approach is based on the collective belief that everyone can learn, change, and improve performance. Research shows that what people believe about their and others' potential has a profound impact on the organization. Whether people have a fixed mindset or a growth mindset seems to make the biggest difference in their capability to learn.

Here's a quick quiz: Who would you rather have on your team?

❐ A high achiever who believes that people either have talent or don't

❐ A person who has a passion for learning and is willing to take risks, make mistakes, and learn from those mistakes

Carol Dweck, a psychology professor at Stanford University, has conducted research and written extensively about the difference between the first response, which is a fixed mindset, and the second, a growth mindset. She suggests that people can be divided into two groups:[5]

1. **Fixed mindset.** A belief that the basic attributes of personality, like intelligence and talent, are fixed and cannot be developed.

2. Growth mindset. A belief that with hard work and learning, the basic attributes of intelligence and talent can be developed and improved.

People with a fixed mindset are inevitably discouraged by failure. They don't recognize that failure is an opportunity for learning. People with a fixed mindset, discouraged by the negative messages sent by their organization, fail to see that every situation is an opportunity to learn because they are constantly judging themselves as failures. A fixed mindset closes the mind to learning and all the possibilities for change and growth.

People with a growth mindset are not discouraged by failure; they are constantly learning from any situation. According to Dweck, "People who believe in the power of talent tend not to fulfill their potential because they're so concerned with looking smart and not making mistakes. But people who believe that talent can be developed are the ones who really push, stretch, confront their own mistakes and learn from them."[6]

The problem is that most performance management systems reinforce the belief that talent is fixed and people cannot change. They fail to encourage development. These systems monitor and measure achievement of goals, but do not track smaller improvements in ability or progress toward goals. In the rapidly changing environments in which people now work, these systems also fail to account for shifting goals, sending the message that the organization only cares about a static set of competencies.

Performance management systems that are based on the talent-is-fixed belief are a barrier to learning. In these systems, individuals are discouraged from admitting failure and exposing their shortcomings. The message employees receive is that if you don't already have the skills and talents needed to move up, your future in the organization is limited. This explains a great deal about the resistance to learning and change evident in many organizations today. A fixed-talent mindset, expressed through the culture of an organization and demonstrated in the behavior of its leaders, prevents people from taking steps to continuously improve themselves, their teams, and the organization as a whole.

Organizational leaders can talk about training, learning, and performance improvement all they want, but unless they confront the underlying beliefs that are a barrier to learning, all that talk will have little impact. Those with a fixed mindset do not develop themselves and do not support the development of others. They do not value training and other types of less formal learning opportunities because they do not believe individuals can learn and change. They do not create and encourage learning experiences because they believe it is a waste of time and resources.

People waste a lot of time and energy on "looking good." Whether high-level executives or frontline employees, they want to be considered smart, competent, and infallible to their managers, organization, and customers. This is a tremendous burden for anyone to carry. None of us can be right and successful all the time, in everything we do. We need to remember the importance of learning from our failures.

Managers who believe that people can learn and develop their abilities support training and other learning solutions. They provide opportunities for individuals to learn and improve themselves. These growth-oriented leaders support the risk taking, experimentation, and stretch assignments that result in more successful individuals and a more successful organization.

But an individual growth mindset is not enough. It must be reflected throughout the culture of the organization. The culture of most organizations sends the message that growth is fixed, which prevents individuals from learning. And without learning, companies are destined to have:

- high turnover
- low-performance teams
- unproductive workplaces
- inadequate responses to competitive pressures
- an inability to keep up with the pace of change
- unsustainable businesses.

So what prevents organizations from managing minds and maintaining a growth mindset focused on learning? Biases cause people to focus too much on success, take action too quickly, try too hard to fit in, and depend too much on experts. These biases lead to short-term, simple solutions to save time and avoid costs. Organizational learning depends on overcoming these biases. Companies must embrace failure and learn to see it as a growth opportunity. They need to take time to reflect on their actions. Companies that embrace failure see and respect nonconformists as individuals whose actions can result in creative solutions to problems. They need to learn to give people opportunities to apply their strengths and learn from one another.[7]

Consider how Microsoft learns from failure. Microsoft CEO Satya Nadella has said, "We need a culture that allows you to constantly renew yourself." In 2016, Tay, a Microsoft chatbot that learned from conversations with users, was taught by Internet trolls to converse using hateful, racist, and misogynistic words. Programmers and others connected to the Tay project held their breath, waiting for their security escort out of the building. But Nadella sent an email that simply told everyone to "keep pushing, and know that I am with you . . . [the] key is to keep learning and improving." It was a great example of not being punished for failure and using it as a chance to learn and get it right.[8]

Companies that manage minds hire for a growth mindset. It's a variation on the idea that you are most affected by the five people you spend most of your day with at work. Are those people helping you learn and grow? Working with a group of people who share a positive growth mindset is enabling. At the end of the day, you feel energized and generally happy about work. But if they are people who waste your time, always provide negative input, are unhappy, and often complain about problems instead of looking for solutions, they'll leave you feeling exhausted and generally unhappy about work. So the overriding question becomes which company do you want to work for? A managing minds company in which people approach work and one another with a growth mindset? Or a company in which people are discouraged and demotivated because of their fixed mindset?

Need for Control

Another barrier to managing minds is leaders' need for control. Managers use short-term, simple solutions, as well as policies, rules, and standards, sometimes for good reason but often out of fear that they will lose control of the situation. This discourages risk taking. As we discussed earlier, a command-and-control structure is one of the hallmarks of a 20th-century industrial economy, managing hands company. Command and control stops creativity and centralizes decision making. The structure erects a wall against the possibility of managing minds because it assumes that the person at the top of the command structure is always right. Open communication is discouraged and reaction to unexpected results is slow, because the flow of information is top-down. Learning is severely limited in an organization where the locus of control is not open to any feedback.

We don't think it's as much a matter of not knowing as it is a fear of losing control. Business leaders today are exposed to every management theory and best practice. However, switching to a people-centered approach means relinquishing control to others and trusting that employees will not abuse that responsibility. This is not easy to do for most managers; only those who are very confident and comfortable in their role can pull it off. And in times of stress, it is human nature to narrow our field of vision and revert to controlling behaviors that feel safe and less risky to us, whether they are or not.

Command and control is not always counterproductive. However, many managers in positions of authority will try to control schedules, output, and budget before they have earned the trust of their employees and peers. Yet while are trying to control everything they can, they want employees to be creative and innovative and to respond rapidly to marketplace changes. The problem is that people won't be creative, innovative, and responsive, and employees won't stay, if they feel disrespected and distrusted by their managers. Managers can't have it both ways.

John Baldoni makes this distinction when he talks about "leadership presence." He argues that it's not enough to have a position of authority; a leader has to earn the trust and respect of followers. This is done through delegating decision making and giving employees the opportunity to implement their own ideas:

Leadership presence is "earned authority." Those two words are important. *Earned* means you have led by example. *Authority* means you have the power to lead others. While organizations confer management roles, it is up to the leader to prove himself or herself by getting others to follow his or her lead. A leader must earn the right to lead others. Title is conferred; leadership is earned. . . . While leaders project power through presence, it is followers who authorize it with their approval.[9]

However, being comfortable enough with who you are that you can relinquish control is not easy. Bureaucratic hierarchies exist for a reason, mostly to give leaders a sense of control over the complexity of the organization. Companies will reorganize ad infinitum to maintain this false sense of control, when the true work of the business is done in the white spaces of the org chart, not inside the lines and boxes.[10]

Work-Learning Dichotomy

A third barrier to managing minds and encouraging learning is the work-learning dichotomy, which is drilled into people at a very young age. Work is what your parents leave home to do someplace else; learning is what you do in school. This mindset is reinforced in college and in the workplace.

When jobs and knowledge changed very slowly, this separation of work and learning might have made sense. Today, work and learning have merged, and it's no longer logical to separate them. With simple, routine tasks being automated and the world of work experiencing rapid change, the jobs that remain require workers to acquire and apply new information and skills quickly and constantly.

However, companies continue to separate work and learning. The obsession with formal training persists. In most companies, training is believed to be the solution to any deficiency in performance, whether at an individual, team, or organization level. Rather than accept responsibility for employee growth, managers relinquish that responsibility to a training department, a CLO, or HR in the hope that they will solve the problem by offering a training program that addresses the issue.

Participation in training is considered a proxy for learning, but we know that real learning requires so much more than formal training. As long as an organization sees training as the solution to all performance problems, it will not take the steps needed for individuals to learn in the current environment.

We do not know what tomorrow will bring, so all workers, from executives to frontline employees, need to continually learn how to adapt what they know to whatever comes at them. And given this need for rapid transformation in an increasingly connected world, learning and adapting are key. Gen. Stanley McChrystal, speaking about the speed of change and interconnectedness of people, says this about continuous learning:

> When you combine the two, speed and interconnectedness, suddenly you have this unpredictability, so you don't know what tomorrow will be like, you don't know what next week, and you certainly don't know next year is like. . . . So you've got to have adaptability to respond to changing conditions . . . it has to be in the DNA of the organization so that it doesn't have to come from top-down directives that say, "Now we are going to produce a new version of this." Instead, it allows the organization to learn, adjust, and adapt automatically.[11]

In this world of increasing speed and interconnectedness, managers must have a growth mindset, believing that everyone can learn and grow and improve with the right kind of support. They must learn how to maintain control by giving responsibility and authority to others. And they must help employees understand that work and learning are not separate activities; learning is their job.

3

COMMUNICATING AND COLLABORATING

FAVI is a French manufacturer and supplier of technical parts for demanding industries with roots in the industrial economy, such as the auto industry. In 1983, former CEO Jean-François Zobrist began to radically change the way the company operated.

As reported by the business blog Corporate Rebels, Zobrist "transformed FAVI from a traditional command-and-control organization to a liberated company based on freedom, trust and equality."[1] He started the move from a rigid hierarchical structure to a flexible communicate-and-collaborate approach by making small yet meaningful changes, including:

- removing the time-clock system
- unlocking all storage rooms, cabinets, and cupboards
- making the beverages in the vending machines free for all employees
- abolishing the annual lunch, which was exclusively held for management

- removing the bonus system, which was too heavily weighted on managers' rewards
- eliminating many departments, such as human resources, planning, and purchasing.

On the surface, these might seem like insignificant, almost symbolic acts. They were in fact the beginning of a dramatic shift in the way the company is run today.

"I was dreaming of a company where the worker would become the operator," Zobrist told Corporate Rebels. "A place where operators would be able to organize themselves, adjust machines themselves and auto-control themselves. . . . At that time, we were only demanding hands and muscles from our employees. . . . I was dreaming of a place where everyone could use his brain and his heart."[2]

The FAVI story has a surprise ending that is in itself instructive. Zobrist decided to retire at a point when FAVI was running smoothly, with low turnover, improved operational performance, and a solid 20 percent net cash flow. When new shareholders took over and moved the company back toward command and control, they lost their best machinists and saw the net cash flow drop to 0 percent. It became a vicious cycle: The more the cash flow fell, the more controls the shareholders put in place, and the more the cash flow dropped. The lesson here is that you can remove command and control successfully, but you cannot put it back once employees have experienced using their minds at work.

Command, but No Control

The command-and-control model for organizations was developed to maintain order in large marching armies with the mission to destroy other large marching armies. This style of management dates back to the Roman Empire, if not earlier. Modern corporations codified this structure to control the numerous hands that needed to be managed. As the Industrial Revolution gained steam, command and control became the accepted approach to building corporations—it was ingrained in the processes and procedures and codified into articles of incorporation used today for old and most new corporations.

A command-and-control manager says:

- "I'm the manager, so I make the rules."
- "Your job is to do what I say."
- "If you mess up, I'll let you know about it."
- "If you don't hear from me, that means you're doing fine."
- "You'd better be careful not to make a mistake or cross me!"
- "Respect for the boss is the most important attribute you can demonstrate."
- "I make the policies, and you follow them."[3]

Guilds and apprenticeships, in which control was more democratic and decentralized, only worked in relatively small organizations of artisans and craftspeople. Most workers today find themselves in command-and-control organizations run by command-and-control managers.

Command and control starts with the decision-making process. When work and workers were still connected to an actual space, leaders felt a need to control distributed decision making. When there are many decisions to be made and many hands to manage, command and control gives leaders a sense that they are in charge of decisions, which will not be made without their input and final say. This approach allows them to justify their importance and remind others of their value to the corporation. But the truth is that the people at the top cannot control everything that goes on in a complex organization.

A command-and-control management style is often the main barrier to corporate learning. This management style prohibits the more open, transparent, and fearless approach that the communicate-and-collaborate model facilitates and supports. Decisions and options often feel predetermined by people at the top and are not open to discussion. Any call for review is too often viewed as unwillingness to be part of the team—a challenge that should be punished. Using training as a reward is the flip side and also symptomatic of this approach.

Deciding to dismantle your company's command-and-control structure takes courage. But trying to maintain the illusion—or delusion—that control in today's knowledge economy is even possible is far more dangerous. You're not alone if you fear that you could commit to reconstructing your organization into one that holds knowledge sharing and collaboration as core values, only to find you have turned it into something that's half fish, half fowl, and can neither swim nor fly.

Fortunately, there is evidence that this does not have to happen. Consider the software development company Nearsoft. Founded in 2007 by Matt Perez and Roberto Martinez, the company has more than 200 employees and has enjoyed rapid growth and increased profits. It also has a highly unusual culture that includes lots of freedom, no managers, and very few rules. Instead, Nearsoft employees rely on a set of five core values: leadership, commitment, teamwork, long-term relationships, and being smart and getting things done.[4]

"We don't believe in command and control," Perez told Corporate Rebels in an interview. "Our people have the freedom and responsibility to make their own decisions . . . and therefore [are] probably more structured than many hierarchical organizations. We have clear processes in place for many things we do."[5]

Perez and Martinez built trial and error into Nearsoft's DNA. "When a person or team wants to experiment with something new, and there is enough internal support, they are completely free to give it a try," said Perez. Once the company decides to try an idea, they commit to it for at least a full year, to give it time to work. And if an experiment fails? No problem: All lessons learned and new information are viewed positively.[6]

Fearless, Not Fearful

With the newer managing minds approach of communication and collaboration, learning is all about acting in ways that are fearless. In the old model, control meant getting the right people to the right event at the right time. Measurement was often limited to the smile sheets handed out at the end of the event to determine if attendees liked what they heard and experienced. The new approach is about making the right information available to whoever needs it when and where it is needed. The measure of success is tied to improvements or increases in performance, or reductions in problems or waste. The locus of learning shifts from the company's training department to managers, individual workers, and their teams.

Real learning, a critical element in a managing minds organization, embraces the possibility of failure and relies on the freedom to act fearlessly. Traci Fenton is founder and CEO of WorldBlu, an organization that promotes and develops "freedom-centered organizations," which is a characteristic of a managing minds company. Fenton got the idea for the organization after working for just four months for a Fortune 500 company. The company's policies made her feel as if she had been stripped of such an unacceptable amount of personal freedom that she quit. Her experience led her to investigate the concepts of personal freedom and democracy, which led her to develop the principles of organizational democracy that are the foundation of WorldBlu.[7]

According to Fenton, the biggest factor that's responsible for sabotaging modern organizations is fear, including fear of failure and uncertainty. She says that asking the simple question, "What would I do if I weren't afraid?" is the key to helping people think big, trust their instincts, take chances, and begin conversations that encourage more freedom and transparency in the workplace.[8]

Yet most businesses shrink from asking questions that will start these conversations. Instead, managers have been programmed to respond to these fears by building control mechanisms into their management process. These mechanisms increase control by decreasing freedom, but they also suppress employees' levels of engagement and initiative. In a global economy, the key to success is being highly agile and responsive, and empowering employees to take initiative. If you think this is an exaggeration, consider that over a three-year period, organizations that have adopted the freedom-centered organizational design and leadership model have realized, on average, 103 percent revenue growth, compared to the S&P Index's 15 percent growth. The average cumulative growth rate for these companies over a three-year period, from 2010 to 2013, was 6.7 times greater than that of the S&P companies that were still mired to one degree or another in their traditional managing hands approach.[9]

The communicate-and-collaborate approach is characterized by a free flow of information and decision making that is top-down, bottom-up, and sideways. This concept is called shared consciousness; it provides everyone with not only the big picture, but also updated details as a situation changes and evolves. Using technology, the entire organization can function like a network in which all the nodes—individuals—are interconnected and sharing information back and forth in real time. In that context, to rapidly learn new information and react creatively, everyone needs to know everything.[10]

We were struck by an image as we wrote about shared consciousness: a pyramid pushing through time and space, and a giant round ball making the same journey (Figure 3-1). The pyramid represents the hierarchical, command-and-control ship that is managing hands, while the ball is the communicate-and-collaborate craft that is managing minds

Figure 3-1. Command and Control vs. Communicate and Collaborate

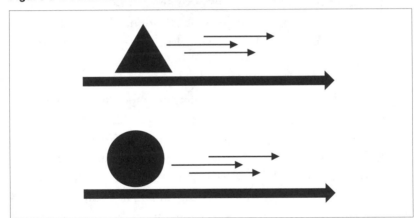

As the pyramid moves along, it encounters turbulence—some problem that causes the commanders in the apex of the pyramid to quickly gather information, react, and make a decision.

That decision is then passed down through all levels of the pyramid to the people working at the base. The people close to and at the bottom of the pyramid have no real idea why they are being asked to react to what the people at the top of the pyramid saw. Thus, they may not do exactly what's required because they are not sure what is going on, and quite honestly, they may not really care as much as their leaders. They won't be fully engaged, and will not bring all their capability and creativity to what they need to do.

The people in the ball are all rolling along; everyone confronts the problem at almost the same time and knows what must be done. These people are managing minds, and each mind is engaged and aware, constantly communicating and collaborating. They feel as if they can innovate, be creative, and work with others to keep the ball rolling. Another way to look at the difference is that leaders pull from the front and bosses push from behind.

A company that keeps the ball rolling is Van Loon Elektrotechniek, a Dutch organization specializing in electrotechnical installations. Rene van Loon founded it about 35 years ago; after merging with competitor Hoppenbrouwers in 2016, it now employs 500 installers. As his company's success grew, Van Loon noticed that his employees seemed to be less and less connected with his passions and dreams for the business. After much thought, Van Loon concluded that because he had founded the company, problems within it were ultimately his responsibility: "I define the culture. When I change personally, the rest will change along, and ultimately the culture of the organization will change."[11]

In 2012, Van Loon turned his company's power pyramid upside down, and gave his employees the responsibility of defining the corporate dream. It took van Loon three months to clearly explain his motives to everyone within the organization. He was completely transparent, giving employees all the information they needed to decide whether they wanted to adopt the changes he proposed.

As might be expected, upending the leadership pyramid has had a dramatic impact on Van Loon Elektrotechniek. The company is now increasing profits year-over-year by 25 percent, and has remarkably low rates of employee sick leave and turnover for that industry. While that level of growth may not be sustainable forever, it is an indication of the boost that can occur when transitioning to managing minds.

Van Loon is understandably happy with these results, but he cautions that working in a company with an employee-driven structure is not as fun as people may think. "The pressure in liberated workplaces is way higher," he says. "There are no options to hide yourself from your responsibilities. And you cannot piggyback on other people's success."

He adds that upending the corporate power pyramid will only work in companies that already have "good infrastructure, good use of technology and a clear purpose" in place.[12]

Similarly, online retail giant Zappos, under the leadership of CEO Tony Hsieh, adopted the holacracy system in 2014. The new system was meant to eliminate bureaucratic hierarchy and shift more control to every employee. In an email to employees, Hsieh wrote that "our main objective is not just to do Holacracy well, but to make Zappos a fully self-organized, self-managed organization by combining a variety of different tools and processes. . . . We won't necessarily adopt all of them, but instead we will experiment and figure out the right tools and processes for Zappos."[13]

Hsieh is making the shift from managing hands to managing minds. He believes that if they can create the right self-management and self-organizing culture, financial success will follow. And he is asking the whole organization to learn with him, to see what will work best for the sustainability of Zappos.[14] So far, they have been very successful.

Like an Open Book

Open-book management (OBM), a phrase coined by *Inc.* magazine's John Case in 1993, exemplifies the difference between a company managing hands and one managing minds. OBM is a way of managing that shares information about how the company is working as a business. Everyone has access to all the financials at any point in time. According to Case, "A company performs best when its people see themselves as partners in the business rather than as hired hands."[15] A company that is managing minds creates this kind of partnership among the people working for the company.

The idea was expanded and turned into a management program, The Great Game of Business, which focused on three basic principles:

1. **Know and teach the rules.** Every employee should be given the measures of business success and taught to understand them.

2. **Follow the action and keep score.** Every employee should be expected and enabled to use their knowledge to improve performance.

3. **Provide a stake in the outcome.** Every employee should have a direct stake in the company's success—and in the risk of failure.[16]

Zingerman's, a specialty food company, has been implementing open-book management with great success. Ari Weinzweig, co-founder and CEO, writes: "[Open-book management] means that we actively share all the financial information about our business with everyone who works within our organization. And that everyone in our organization, from dishwashers on down the line to owners and accountants, is responsible for the financial performance of the organization."[17]

OBM has helped Zingerman's improve finances, service, product quality, and staff morale. The company believes it is the right thing to do because it is in line with company values, builds employee commitment, and helps them make better decisions. But it is still learning about OBM and making improvements. Weinzweig puts this in perspective: "Ten years on, I can say that we're most definitely still learning about this relatively modern approach to money and organizational life. But given that it's a work in progress I can tell you that I believe more strongly than ever that open book finance has been, and will continue to be, the right way for us to go."[18]

When you manage the minds of the people who work in the organization, you ask them to bring their intelligence, experience, education, curiosity, skills, dreams, and hopes to work every day. And then, as with OBM, you give them the opportunity to apply their thinking to the business of the organization. It's one way to put the "force" back into workforce.

Output—work—in a managing minds environment is much harder to measure and count. The old way of managing hands depended on time and space—for example, the physical presence of workers, products, and service calls, and the measures of time to performance, time and motion numbers, and time clocks. We need a new way to measure, one that accounts for new consumption habits based on the digital reality, and we need a new way to look at productivity in organizations.

There is an interesting analogy with a corporate P&L and a country GDP that relates to the command-and-control structure of a company. In 2016, HSBC Economist James Pomeroy published "The Rise of the Digital Natives," a thought-provoking piece that looked at the consumption patterns of people born into an always-on digital world. His idea is that the old way of measuring GDP—actual goods and measurable services—is not an accurate measure of wealth now and will be even less so in the future. The reason is that many digital goods and services bought today are virtual.[19]

A Melding of the Minds

In the old managing hands model, a manager decided what people needed to learn and told them to go learn it, and then get back to work. In the new managing minds model, a manager needs to be able to discover what each person really needs to know, and then collaborate with that employee to find different ways to make the information available in ways that fit how that person prefers to learn. This requires a careful touch.

In the Vulcan language, it was known as *taroon-ifla*, the Vulcan mind meld. The mind meld was a wonderful piece of fiction invented by Gene Roddenberry for his 1960s *Star Trek* television series. The mind meld is a telepathic technique used by Vulcans, in which the minds of two individuals become one. In a culture in which managing minds is the key to success, Spock would have made a great manager. He would have the capability to quickly discover what people knew about their work, what they needed to know, and when and where that knowledge was needed.

Fortunately, you don't have to be a mind reader to discover the knowledge and skills people need to do their jobs. A managing minds company is one that focuses on continuous learning. There is an ongoing, two-way flow of information about what people know, what they need to know, and, ideally, what they do not yet know they need to know. Managers discover what people need to learn by listening and observing. People can tell a manager when there is a problem or if they see something new coming at the company. Managers, in collaboration with employees, can then determine what needs to be learned and the best way for knowledge and skills to be shared. It may not be as easy as the mind meld, but the alternative, command and control, no longer works to make the company smarter.

Cyberclick is a company headquartered in Barcelona, Spain, and was rated the best company in Spain to work for in 2014 and 2015.[20] It's also an example of a company that is part of the worldwide movement of companies trying to manage minds. David Tomas, CEO and founder, is trying to reinvent the way he and the people at Cyberclick work. It starts with the values of the company, which are determined by the employees themselves, the essence of a collaborate-and-communicate approach. Furthermore, once a week the teams gather together and hold a stand-up meeting, during which all employees give an example of how they experienced one of the values that week.

Goals in Cyberclick are bottom-up. First, employees set their personal goals. The company goals are then drawn from these goals and the two are aligned, the exact opposite of the command-and-control approach used in managing hands companies.

Because continuous learning is a key value, employees get an individual training budget and can spend it on whatever they like, from theoretical quantum physics to scuba-diving lessons. And every three months, employees read a book they all think is worthwhile, and discuss the book together at work. Cyberclick believes that learning, as long as it is good for personal development, is good for the company.

They measure their happiness through a short daily survey. This used to be anonymous, but the employees changed this because of the high amount of trust they have for one another. The scores are discussed on a weekly basis. If a very unhappy score shows up, it's discussed immediately. Only when the problem is solved do employees continue with their work.

Cyberclick works with open-book management. Everyone gets training to understand the basic financials of the company, and there's complete transparency. As with other OBM companies, employees feel and act like partners in the business; all the minds that are being managed can actively watch the numbers and see what needs the most attention and when.[21]

Know What, Why, How, and Who

There have been numerous attempts at using technology to manage knowledge that have hit roadblocks for two basic reasons. The first is that the technology is too cumbersome. The user experience is filled with logins, approvals, caveats, and an overload of irrelevant information. Managing minds is enabled by technology, but it is always driven by people who need information. The simpler and easier the technology is to get the job done, the better. The second reason is more complex: Our habits, attitudes, and a profound failure of the imagination create roadblocks to managing knowledge.

Here's a short quiz. Check all the answers that apply to the way you share the four types of knowledge—know-what, know-why, know-how, and know-who:[22]

Know-What

- ❏ You manage a team and give out information on what you consider to be a need-to-know basis.
- ❏ You cannot be bothered to collaborate; you already have more than enough to do.
- ❏ You simply are too busy and forget to check in and share what you learned.
- ❏ You do not trust anyone in your company, because they are out to get you if you raise your hand and offer an idea.

Know-Why

- ❏ Your project seems successful and you want to quickly move on without hearing any bad news before it all falls apart.
- ❏ You learned that if anyone says anything negative it rocks the boat, and you've learned to go along to get along.
- ❏ You have learned to grab short-term gains and run before long-term losses catch-up.

Know-How

- ❏ You think your ideas will be laughed at and put down; you avoid any forum where that could happen.

☐ You've had good ideas in the past but no one paid much attention, so you gave up.

☐ You feel safe being invisible and never raise your hand, because they cannot shoot you if they cannot see you.

☐ You believe knowledge is like money; the more you have, the better you can do and get what you want.

☐ When you know what's happening, you enjoy the feeling of having power over people who you think are clueless.

Know-Who

☐ You already made a decision and are looking for people to agree with what you decided.

☐ You have read the news for the last few years and learned not to trust senior management.

☐ Raises, promotions, bonuses, and pats on the back all depend on how much knowledge you know that no one else knows.

☐ Being on the inside track is the best place to be, and you do not want to share what you know with too many other people.

☐ You like knowing what others don't know because it makes you feel important.

☐ You want to be one of the cool people who are smart and in-the-know and protect the knowledge wealth you acquire.

It's a long list, the result of years of habits and attitudes created in companies that focused on managing hands. If you checked off most of the boxes, we're not surprised. The cure? Start to manage minds and find new ways you can communicate and collaborate.

The following are some ideas we learned from the managing minds companies we studied. Make a list of the ones you can do today. Turn them into posters for everyone to read. Keep adding more until you start to create your own.

You can begin by teaching people to respectfully listen to all ideas. Stop saying phrases such as, "It's the way we always do it here," "It's none of your business," or, "It's above your pay grade." Those are great ways to stop minds in their tracks. It's exciting to start managing minds because the result is controlled conflict, chaos, and controversy. Keep it nice, but keep it interesting.

In a managing minds company, you need to start promoting people who learn, teach, and share what they know throughout the year. Live the idea that sharing knowledge is the real power. Teach everyone in the company how to genuinely and respectfully teach what they know and know how to do. Provide incentives other than money for people who freely share important knowledge throughout the year. Give recognition to the people who provide good ideas that the company uses. Make the recognition as public and frequent as possible. And whatever you do, stop telling people, "It's OK to say what you're thinking," and then punishing the person for saying it. Word spreads like wildfire when that happens and people stop thinking.

Support knowledge sharing by putting easy-to-use tools in place that enable that behavior. One of the keys to collaboration and communication is making sure it's easy to do and freely available to everyone. Encourage different ways of sharing knowledge—weekly group discussions, mentoring, coaching, videos of something new, photographs before and after—all in the name of open sharing of the four types of knowledge: the what, why, how and who.

As our research and examples prove, becoming a managing minds company starts with leadership at the top. Move away from the corner office and stop controlling the flow of information about the company and the company's financials. Use the principles and practices found in open-book management. Share with employees as much as possible about how they—for they are the company—are doing financially. Most important, make managing the company mind an integral part of everyone's job with all it entails.

Companies around the world that are successfully managing minds are finding the following:
- more impact from learning solutions
- faster time to performance
- improved job growth and satisfaction
- greater innovation and creativity
- more agile problem solving

- faster and better decisions
- increased savings.

It's what you are in business to do; you just need a better way of doing it.

4

PUSHING AND PULLING

To manage minds and not hands, you need to discard the old dichotomy of formal training and informal learning. This arbitrary distinction is not very helpful in a managing minds world. We believe a more useful distinction is whether learning is push or pull.

Before you can begin to transform your organization into one that manages minds, you need to acknowledge that most people are not going to learn what they need to be most efficient on the job in a traditional "push" training setting, whether it is a one-hour class, a two-day seminar, or an e-learning program. Instead, learning is a continuous process. What is learned becomes evident and measurable over time. It cannot be measured from Level 1 assessment forms collected at the end of a class.[1] You must be willing to seriously commit both time and money to change the existing push training model to a pull learning culture, where continuous learning is the norm, expected, and fully supported.

What does a company look like when it has successfully evolved from a number of separate departments primarily responsible for pushing training into an integrated pull learning model supporting an entire company? Figures 4-1 and 4-2 show the difference between the old, unaligned push training culture, and the new, aligned pull model for learning.

Figure 4-1. The Old Push Model

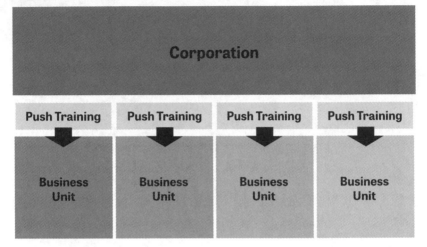

In the same way that IT departments started out being tied to a business unit and realized it was more effective and efficient to centralize and work across the enterprise, push training and learning needs to consolidate. To support the new managing minds organization, training departments need to be centralized into an enterprise-wide learning group.

Push training is a siloed, top-down, management-driven approach that sends people to formal training events where they receive nice-to-know information—as in, it will be nice to know someday. People are not connected to one another during or after the training event, and do not collaborate. The focus is on showing up (attendance), participating (raising your hand), and passing or failing (testing). If that sounds familiar, that's because it's school transposed onto the workplace. It is a static system created to control and manage hands.

Figure 4-2. The New Pull Model

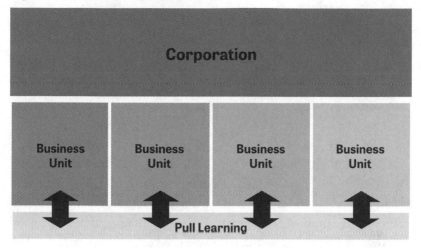

In contrast, pull learning is a learner-driven, bottom-up approach that enables people to access the information they need when and where it is needed. People are able to collaborate and make the best use of the supporting technology that links them to one another and sources of information. The focus is on performance (what you can do), sharing knowledge that leads to better performance (collaborating), and providing two-way feedback about the information that affects what others will learn (communicating).

Imagine people facing a new situation in which they require more instruction. Using the push model, no one is sure where to go to get the information they need. They attended a training program, but it did not cover all the possible situations they would encounter, and they have already forgotten most of the content. With pull learning, people can quickly and easily locate and access the most up-to-the-minute information in a variety of ways, when and where they need it. They can call a co-worker who has already learned what is needed, talk to an expert, or search an interactive site for the latest ideas from other people. The pull model of learning is performance-based. The focus is on what you can do when you need to get it done. Table 4-1 summarizes these key differences.

Table 4-1. Push and Pull

Push Training Culture	Pull Learning Culture
Event-based learning	On-demand learning
Delayed response to changing needs	Immediate response
Knowing	Doing
Instructor-centered	Learner-centered
Delivery of programs	Delivery of results
Top-down centralized	Bottom-up decentralized

Replacing push training with pull learning is a transformative step toward supporting and sustaining a company. It is managing minds and placing a mission-critical value on learning. By taking a managing minds approach, a company can provide relevant, usable, and on-demand access to the knowledge and skills people need to perform their jobs. This includes technical, operational, and managerial knowledge and skills.

Corporations that make the commitment to manage minds and emphasize pull learning experience measurable, significant, and sustainable increases in on-the-job performance, talent-retention, sales revenue, and innovation.[2] They are more agile, and more able to respond instantly to the ever-changing requirements and demands of a fast-paced, hypercompetitive marketplace. Their employees can quickly access the technology and support to find what they need to know, when and where it is needed.

Learning and Doing

Shifting from training and knowing to learning and doing improves the thousands of job-related actions and decisions performed each day, and makes mission-critical corporate-level decisions more immediate and effective. Decision making is quickly informed and validated by the people most in need of learning. As many corporations are discovering, the best solutions are made by the people closest to the problem.

In a managing hands training culture, every learning deficit looks like a nail to the training hammer. But managers have access to many different ways beyond training to facilitate learning:

- Executive coaching might be a better way for some people to develop leadership skills.
- Action learning might be a better way for some groups to learn how to improve project management.
- A computer simulation might be a better way for some workers to learn safety procedures.
- Getting performance feedback while operating a new machine might be a better way of learning how to operate that machine.
- Observing an organization go through a strategic planning process and then reflecting on that process might be a better way for people to learn about strategic planning.

It's important to note that push and pull are not mutually exclusive. Learning solutions in a company managing minds range from traditional classroom push training programs to on-the-job, just-in-time knowledge pulled by people when and where it is needed. The key is that the people doing the work decide which learning solution or blend of solutions to use, based on what they need to learn.

These companies think of push training and pull learning as a process. First, training introduces or reintroduces people to the baseline knowledge, skills, attitudes, and beliefs they need. Then, pull methods reinforce, extend, amplify, and sustain those abilities until individuals, teams, and organizations have attained the level of mastery needed by the company. It is not about training; it's about learning and using the best methods to produce measurable performance gains.

Push training, and the attendant tracking, might be necessary to meet the legal, compliance, and regulated safety requirements of an external agency. However, even in this case, learning is enhanced by pull learning back in the workplace. Safety training, compliance, HR training, and regulatory or legal issues are like learning a new language. The basic vocabulary, syntax, definitions, and usage are critical to gaining more complex knowledge and know-how in these topics. So push training about the basics gives everyone the common language they need to then pull what they need to know and know how to do when they are back at work. It's much more effective to pull the relevant information when it's needed than try and remember the training session that gave you everything someone thought you might need to know someday.

The Forgetting Curve

Let's examine this from another vantage point and take a look at the learning process. In a company that is only managing hands, information is pushed at people, and they go back to work as soon as the in-person or online program is finished. The expectation is that they can do their jobs as a result of their training. They are getting just-in-case training.

We know from research on forgetting that push training is not sufficient. As far back as 1885, during the early part of the industrial economy, researchers wondered why training did not immediately meet the expectations for improved performance. Hermann Ebbinghaus extrapolated the hypothesis of the exponential nature of forgetting. The following formula roughly describes it: $R = e - S / t$, where R is memory retention, S is the relative strength of memory, and t is time.[3]

A typical graph of the forgetting curve shows that we tend to halve our memory of newly learned knowledge in a matter of days or weeks unless we consciously review what we learned (Figure 4-3). Yet we have persisted for more than 100 years in using the push training approach as the only way to learn.

Figure 4-3. The Forgetting Curve

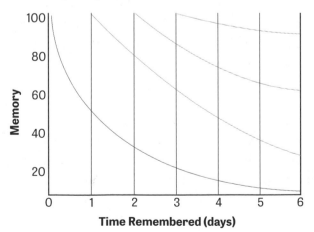

Research at IBM in the late 1980s showed that a disproportionate amount of learning—between 70 and 80 percent—takes place on the job, in the course of your work.[4] The implications are eye-opening. If training programs account for only 20 to 30 percent of learning (if learners remember), then employees are entering the workplace with 70-80 percent left to learn. When these events are, for example, focused on safety procedures, it's unsettling to imagine the results when we send people back to work having learned only 20-30 percent of what they need to know about safety procedures, which could endanger their lives and the lives of others. Yet that represents industrial economy workplaces that are still managing hands with push training.

In a company that is managing minds, training, when it is needed, is designed to catapult the learner into the more critical period of pull learning. We imagine a future in which post-training could reinforce push training and provide the needed information whenever and wherever it was most useful. Instead of just-in-case training, employees would be getting just-in-time learning.

To get to this point now, training programs should include ways that people can use pull learning to overcome the steep forgetting curve and help people remember what was taught. For example, a push training program could emphasize many of the following ideas:

- explaining why a course or program needs to be learned and used
- listing and applying key takeaways from the push training program
- using push training materials on the job
- making best use of job aids
- getting access to, and help from, experts when needed
- repeating and practicing basic procedures from training
- collaborating with others around the knowledge and skills that were learned
- having employees teach what they know to others
- reviewing what employees have learned at set times.

Looking at this list, the implications for change between the old and new models for managing learning are significant. The old push model delivers training and stops cold. The managing minds approach uses push training as a beginning, a jumping-off point for pull learning. Push training programs would be the first step in the learning process, and would be more focused on preparing people and laying the groundwork for the skills they need to test and use. Learning is a process of adapting and adopting. Learners adopt the lessons they derive from a push training program. They then adapt those lessons through a self-managed process of trying, failing, succeeding, and learning from experience, during a constantly changing set of circumstances. The new pull model would account for the new "three Rs": Review, reinforce, and remember. Here are three examples of elements of a hybrid pull model:

- interactive performance support (IPS)
- new e-learning systems—xAPI and learning record store
- from push to pull—the pivot point.

Interactive Performance Support

Performance support, introduced by Gloria Gery in 1991 as electronic performance support systems (EPSS), is the antidote to forgetting. It places the information people might need to know about operations, repair, maintenance, or compliance at the point of greatest need.

The first time we encountered an EPSS was in a Polaroid manufacturing plant in Massachusetts. It was attached to the pod-making machine and was a series of color-coded plastic index cards on a stand, which evolved into a computer program that displayed answers to operators' questions. If an employee needed to quickly find out what to do when the secret green goo that developed the Polaroid picture needed to be refilled, the card explained what to do. It was the training program information when you needed it just-in-time.

The most up-to-date version is what we call interactive performance support. KnowledgeStar is an example of how an IPS program could be employed in a manufacturing environment.

You're walking over to your industrial-grade, high-precision CNC lathe, and your cellphone buzzes to get your attention. The lathe has been equipped with a near-field communication beacon, which sent you a text: "The lathe needs a compliance check today. Here is the checklist. Please complete the checklist and send it back to Susan before noon." Susan is back at corporate in the compliance department. As you approach the machine, the checklist pops up on your smartphone waiting to be completed.

At the fourth item on the list, you're not sure you remember what exactly needs to be done—you have fallen off the Forgetting Curve. So you go to the lathe's instructions and operations page on your phone and watch a short video—taken from your push training class—on how to make sure the vector control spindle drive is correctly calibrated. You watch the video as it plays on your smartphone, pausing at each step, and follow the instructions. The exact procedure must be done right, and so you want to make sure you understand how to do it correctly. You then use your phone to locate another employee who has been tagged as an expert on doing this job. She answers your call and explains exactly what you need to watch out for when you do the calibration, and stays on the phone until you are finished with that part of the process. Once the calibration is done, you snap a photo, finish checking the boxes on the list, and send the photo and the completed list back to Susan.

An IPS program can:
- Reduce downtime.
- Increase time to performance.
- Increase return on investment for machine manufacturers.
- Increase productivity.
- Reduce injuries and accidents.
- Provide better compliance.
- Deliver more up-to-date information.
- Improve communication and collaboration.

This is one example of the way technology can support the work of people who are being asked to use their minds.

E-Learning Systems

In a company focused on managing minds, learning comes at you from all directions. It can be push, pull, mobile, or social, resulting from mentoring, coaching, networking, team, or work experiences that a learning management system (LMS) was never created to track and manage. It is therefore more difficult to integrate what people are learning into a coherent story about what they know and know how to do. It is also harder to make assignments and pull teams together. Fortunately, Experience API (xAPI) can solve these problems.

xAPI is a specification used by programmers for software programs. Once xAPI is programmed into a software program or web portal and someone uses the program or portal for learning, it generates xAPI data—a record of what people have learned—that is stored in a new database called a learning record store (LRS). It's important to keep in mind that LMSs only manage and track e-learning programs, while the LRS can be used for any type of learning that has been tagged with the xAPI specification. The LRS can function separately, or it can work with the LMS to form a more complete picture of what each person is learning.

xAPI tracks what people are doing using activity streams, the same way that sites such as Google and Facebook know what you are looking at, reading, shopping for, and buying. Those activity-stream trackers are the source of all those related popup boxes that appear as you browse. But in this case, what's being tracked are learning programs.

Here is an example. John has been working at his company as a writer in the marketing and communications department for six months. The company is in a crunch, the sales people are maxed out, and a sales proposal needs to be written to a new customer for one of their products by next week. John, a great marketing copywriter, has some experience with proposals, and has been looking for the opportunity to do more. He volunteers to do the job.

There is a company that offers an online proposal writing course that John's manager has taken and rated highly. The program guides learners through a series of writing assignments, and shows them how to develop a sales proposal for a new product. The assignments are reviewed and discussed on the phone with a seasoned proposal writer.

John gets started on the course that is initially delivered and tracked by the LMS. The company's learning portal, which delivers the writing assignments, is set up to handle xAPI data in an LRS and track his learning activities—including assignments, phone calls, and any resulting work that comes out of the reviewer's comments. The LMS and LRS capture the following progress as John learns to be a sales proposal writer:

LMS

- completes the six lessons in the Proposal Writing for Beginners course
- passes the exams at the end of each lesson
- successfully completes the proposal writing assignment at the end of the course.

LRS

- logs onto the sales portal and signs up for the writing assignment program
- takes account of each of the seven writing assignments
- shows how each assignment was reviewed by a sales proposal writing coach
- logs the revisions for each assignment based on feedback from the coach
- takes note of the recommended and completed reading for several websites on writing winning sales proposals
- captures the final assignment, a draft of the actual sales proposal reviewed by his manager
- makes a note of the fact that the deal was closed as a result of the proposal.

John's learning process can be reviewed at any point by his manager. The LMS delivers and tracks the traditional e-learning program on proposal writing that got him started. At that point, were it not for xAPI, the more complete level of the knowledge he gained would have been lost. Because his work was tracked using xAPI through the company learning portal, the assignments and coaching developed by the company, the recommended website reading, the final review by the manager, and the outcome from his learning and work were all documented. The next time someone is looking for a writer to deliver a winning sales proposal, John can be tapped as someone who has successfully learned how to do the job.

There are three very valuable reasons xAPI is a key technology in a company managing minds. The first is the obvious advantage of being able to track all the learning inputs that someone has to blend push and pull into the entire learning process. Until xAPI, much of what people learned was invisible. Coaching and mentoring, information gathered from websites, attendance at conferences and workshops, and self-directed reading were reported anecdotally, if at all. xAPI gives people a record they can share that highlights what they are learning.

The second is the chance to really develop people. Providing the opportunity to connect push and pull learning to actual work assignments and achievements offers exciting new opportunities for companies to really know what people can do. It is a more precise guide to planning, developing, and helping people advance their careers.

Finally, for the people responsible for developing these xAPI-based programs, xAPI offers a new window into the development of holistic learning programs. They can now see from the outcomes what is working and what needs to be improved. If John could not write a winning proposal after all the work he did, they can discover why and make a course correction. If the total learning experience is working, it can be used by other people trying to learn the same skill. It's a chance to manage minds in ways that truly connect push and pull learning.

The Pivot Point

When the starting gun goes off, learners eagerly follow the instructor around the learning track. The critical question becomes, "Do they make the leap to the workplace?" You need to identify the switch from push training to pull learning, and create a bridge between the two. To manage this bridge, you need to understand the "pivot point."

The pivot point is the moment push training ends and pull learning needs to begin. A training course can take the Ebbinghaus Forgetting Curve into account, providing the tools to reinforce the basics upon which learners can build. Focusing training on the pivot point is important for several reasons:

- Learners need to be aware of what is involved when they pivot from push training to pull learning.
- The focus on the pivot point will make sure employees' training is supported when they return to the workplace.

- A plan for a well-timed hand-off from the push side to the pull side can be developed to support employee performance during their informal learning.
- Push training events can be designed to mirror the environment in which learners will work to make the pivot as seamless as possible.
- This approach will reinforce the new goal of training: to prepare learners to successfully pivot and apply their newly learned skills when they are back at work.

No one brings the same level of skills to a training program. Yet a push training program can still be one-size-fits-all. Everyone will need certain basics as they move from the push to the pull part of the learning process. Those basics can be covered in ways to help bridge the transition between the two parts of the learning process.

In Figure 4-4, the initial learning curve represents the research done by Ebbinghaus and others. There is a precipitous drop in what someone learns during the push training program. During the learning process, learning peaks at the pivot point, toward the end of the push training program. If nothing happens past the pivot point, people start to drop off the curve and forget what they learned.

At the pivot point, pull learning needs to take over. This may be toward the end of the push training program, even as learners are still in class completing a survey or a smile sheet. People need to adapt, test, and expand upon what they've learned and go through a series of similar, shorter learning curves until reaching a level of mastery.

The learning process can be summed up as a series of curves, each one representing the need to adopt, test, and adapt what we learn. Each of these later learning curves, where more complex or sophisticated learning is tried, also has a downward side, where there is a falling off or forgetting of new information. The difference is that each succeeding curve in this extended learning process becomes less steep. We remember more, forget less, and need to learn less next time. As people draw closer to an expert level, the curve is almost a straight line. The key is to allow for time and reinforcement new skills and behaviors in the real context in which they are needed.

Figure 4-4. The Pivot Point and the Learning Process

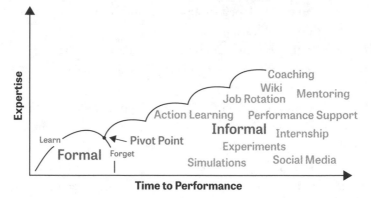

Golf is a useful illustration of the learning process, in which the ongoing learning curves flatten over time. Let's say you want to learn to play golf. You go to a seminar, read a book about the history and etiquette of golf, and watch a videotape of great golfing moments. You can now say you know something about golf. But have you really learned how to play golf?

You then buy and enjoy a great e-golf game, find a golf pro, take lessons, and practice your swing and putting, slicing and hooking balls at the driving range all weekend. After all this, have you really learned how to play golf?

From your first tee shot on your first hole, it takes hours of adopting and adapting, alone or in a foursome, in all sorts of weather conditions. You discover what you know and can do, swing all the clubs, ask all sorts of questions, fail and succeed, practice and practice some more, before you have really learned to play golf. Real learning, then, is the state of being able to adopt and adapt what you know and can do—what you have acquired through formal event-driven learning—under a varying set of informal, constantly changing circumstances.[5]

Many different learning solutions, some push and some pull, can be used to facilitate learning around the pivot point. First, managers can help learners decide what needs to be learned. Then, they can help learners choose the method or combination of methods that will contribute to that learning. Here is a list of some of the most commonly used methods. The first five are primarily instructor directed (push); the second five are primarily learner directed (pull).

Instructor Directed:

- **instructor-led, classroom instruction:** face-to-face lectures, seminars, workshops, and e-learning programs
- **coaching and mentoring:** relationships in which leaders help employees develop the knowledge and skills needed to be more effective in their jobs
- **games and simulations:** experiences that make learning interactive and fun by applying the principles of gaming, such as scoring, competition, and rules of play, to replicating real-life problem solving within a virtual and safe environment
- **external conferences, lectures, and courses:** participating in outside events intended for professional development, sometimes provided by leading institutions and from renowned faculty
- **internships, apprenticeships, and job rotation:** working in a temporary position to learn about a job, the work environment, and the organizational culture.

Learner Directed:

- **action learning:** learning from reflecting on an activity while doing it, from reflecting on an activity by looking back on what happened, and by applying what was learned in a past situation to a new situation
- **daily log:** individual employees writing or recording learning from each day of work and then discussing their observations with co-workers
- **experiments:** gathering evidence in a controlled environment to support or refute a particular change that is being proposed, such as prototyping an innovation in the product development process and then trying it out with a few customers and learning from what happens
- **learning communities:** people who share the same interests or responsibilities in an organization, or across organizations, come together to learn from one another

- **interactive performance support program:** web-based materials that provide information about a specific task that are accessed just-in-time.

The pivot point is at the heart of a managing minds organization. Training programs in this environment can no longer be seen as the end of learning before working, but as the gateway to performing at the highest level.

When we start to see learning as a continuous process from push to pull (and sometimes circling back over and over again), we realize the value of the pivot point. And we realize that with planning, we can make that pivot a seamless move from pushing knowledge and skills to people pulling what they need, when they need it, where it's needed. The pivot point is an opportunity to start managing minds that does not require any new technology during or after the learning event. Connecting the push training and pull learning opens the door to a more complete learning experience.

5

CONTINUOUS LEARNING

In the 20th century, when hands made things and we needed to manage those hands, there was time to learn. We measured the shelf-life of knowledge in months, sometimes even years. We had time to shadow someone for years to really move from apprentice to master or go to a course to learn something that you might need someday. Products and services changed slowly, and even when they did it was incremental. Disruption had not yet entered the conversation.

In the 21st-century knowledge economy, work is produced by minds and we are quickly learning how to manage them. We've realized that everything is changing more quickly; even the pace of change is rapidly increasing. The idea of learning something someday or soon no longer works. We base our new model of learning on the idea of now, as in, "I need to learn it now," "Tell me how to do it now," and, "I want that information now." Googling has replaced dictionaries. Facebook and Twitter have replaced message boards to a degree. LinkedIn has connected professionals from all parts of the globe. Slack instantly pulls all the pieces and people together into working teams. Other apps provide the connective tissue to help people form a digital community.

There is a moment in the movie *The Matrix* when Trinity says, "I need to know how to fly a helicopter!" She plugs a jack directly into her brain and downloads the skills. Plugging in to what she needed to learn was as direct and fast as the screenwriters could imagine.

In a sense, we have the ability to plug in now; we just fail to maximize it or rarely use it to form communities that help employees learn and practice. Any learning solution that involves two or more people can be connected. That connected community enables learners to network, collaborate, and get used to the idea of a technology-mediated community in which learning is the focus. Making sure that everyone in the organization can connect using any number of devices enables people to ask for and receive just-in-time information that will help them continuously improve performance. It is one of the key characteristics of a managing minds organization.

A manager's role in the knowledge economy must include support for just-in-time, on-demand learning, whether that involves training programs or any of the many other ways in which people learn. Here are some different ways you can help facilitate continuous learning.

Self-Directed Learning

Google is committed to continuous learning. The company established Google Fridays, when employees can pursue any topic they want to explore or research. This implies another set of behaviors necessary for managing minds: enabling everyone to be a self-directed learner.

In a managing minds company, it is critical that employees take responsibility for their own learning, pulling the information they need when and where they need it. Malcolm Knowles, a leader in the field of adult learning, defined this as self-directed learning:

> In its broadest meaning, self-directed learning describes
> a process in which individuals take the initiative, with or
> without the help of others, in diagnosing their learning needs,
> formulating learning goals, identifying human and material

resources for learning, choosing and implementing appropriate learning strategies, and evaluating learning outcomes.[1]

Self-directed learners are people who get intrinsic rewards from their ability to locate, curate, share, and communicate what they have learned independently. Extrinsic rewards—more money, awards and plaques, additional perks and power—might have worked in the industrial economy, but in a knowledge economy, intrinsic rewards work best. Creating an environment in which people who are self-directed learners can achieve those intrinsic rewards is essential.

According to Daniel Pink, there are three key elements necessary to create this environment.[2] The first is the ability to work when and where an employee wants; no micromanaging allowed! Minds can work in an office space or a virtual space. A level of autonomy is necessary for people to do their best work. Being left alone with the problem or challenge and having the freedom to work it out is the best way to kick-start the self-directed learner's process.

Second, self-directed learners must believe that it is a stretch to get from the problem to the solution. They live for the challenge that makes them draw upon as many parts of their brain as they can to pull the rabbit out of the hat. Straining their resources as they reach for the solution to a problem is energizing, and provides a sense of mastery over the subject.

The third element is finding a sense of purpose in what they are doing. Working in the service of a larger mission or goal completes the trifecta for a self-directed learner. Pink uses the example of programmers providing open source code for no pay because they were motivated by the idea of providing free software for the world. Autonomy, mastery, and purpose enable and empower the self-directed learner.

While we believe that people should take full responsibility for their own learning, we also recognize that many people do not have this ability. They need to move from a fixed mindset to a growth mindset. They need to learn how to learn independently and get over years of learning in an educational system that spoon-fed them what they were supposed to learn. They will need help identifying their learning needs, finding and using resources (including computer technology), practicing and reinforcing learning, and evaluating results.

What if the people working for you are not yet self-directed? In this case, your responsibility is to help them learn how to learn. People need guidance and support from their managers to become self-directed. Every manager has a key role to play in making it possible for their direct reports to develop the knowledge and skills they need to be successful in their work. Managers need to set the expectation for self-directed learning and then create the conditions for people to learn independently. The complementary roles of managers and employees can follow a structure similar to the one in Table 5-2.

Table 5-2. Managers and Learners in Self-Directed Learning

Manager Role	Learner Role
Have a growth mindset	Develop a growth mindset
Hire for ability and motivation to learn	Be actively learning how to learn
Help learners identify strengths and weaknesses	Identify personal strengths and weaknesses
Encourage employee learning	Learn continuously
Make it safe to learn	Take risks and learn from successes and failures
Create opportunities for people to learn individually and in groups	Take advantage of opportunities to learn as individuals, and with and from others
Make technology available to learners	Learn how to use technology to learn
Give feedback effectively	Receive feedback effectively
Co-create and co-curate information with learners	Co-create and co-curate information with their managers
Convey high expectations for learning	Strive to do their best and exceed expectations of managers
Recognize and reward learning	Use recognition and rewards to further learning

The relationship between managers and their employees needs to start with a growth mindset. This belief needs to be shared by managers and employees. You want people who make learning part of the way they work, who are constantly assessing their strengths and weaknesses and seeking out the knowledge and skills that will position them to be more successful. Managers should encourage this and create a safe environment where people can be open about their strengths and weaknesses without being criticized or judged.

You want opportunities for people to learn, and apply newly acquired knowledge and skills to important work on the job. People can arrange some opportunities for themselves, but this requires managers to give permission, make time, and provide the resources to apply what they learn.

According to a 2014 Gallup poll, managers who cannot or will not provide feedback "fail to engage 98 percent of employees."[3] That's not a typo—98 percent. You need to give performance feedback in a helpful and productive way. You want people to hear and understand that feedback and make use of it to learn and improve their performance. This must be more than an annual performance review. Performance feedback, positive and negative, should be given at every opportunity throughout the year.

Managers should have high but realistic expectations for the people with whom they work. People should be clear about these expectations and how they are linked to performance. This gives them a clear direction and path to performance improvement, which motivates learning and the application of that learning.

Managers should recognize and reward the impact of what people learn on achieving the goals of the organization. This could include public statements about the learner's success, a promotion, new responsibilities, or special compensation. Whatever it is, learners need to see clearly how what they learned resulted in this expression of appreciation. The key is to publicly acknowledge the way learners (individuals and teams) have adopted and adapted knowledge to make the company smarter.

When self-directed learning is valued by an organization, you can expect to see the following:

- A salesperson in the field preparing to make a presentation to a client quickly and easily access the most recent information about a product and service.

- A lathe operator in a manufacturing plant, unsure about the correct FPM (cutting speed) and RPM (spindle speed) for a job, quickly gets this information before he begins.
- An employee traveling in another country quickly locates the minutes of the last company board meeting for use in a speech he's writing.
- The foreman of an HVAC crew is working on a high-rise and needs to verify part of the city's building code. He immediately accesses the names and numbers of three experts he can contact who are authorized to tell him how to proceed.
- A manager is about to have a performance-review meeting with one of her direct reports. She goes to the company's internal wiki and finds suggestions for how to conduct a productive performance review session.
- A team leader is having difficulty keeping team members engaged in their work. She meets with other team leaders to discuss effective ways for engaging team members.

Harold Jarche, one of the most outstanding thinkers and writers about organizational learning, emphasizes the critical need for companies to develop and support self-directed learners: "Management needs to support self-learning. . . . Workers will also have to be their own instructional designers."[4] Managers, in companies managing minds, play an important role in helping people develop self-directed learning skills, including curation, critical thinking, effective communication, active participation, self-reflection, creativity, and emotional intelligence.

Curation

It's fair to say that a universal dilemma of the 21st century is too much information, too little time. We are inundated with email, tweets, blog posts, LinkedIn updates, and Facebook messages, in addition to traditional media such as newspapers, magazines, TV, and radio. Because of the overwhelming amount of information available, people need the skills to choose what information to process. They need to be able to focus on a small set of information, separate out the noise, and judge its accuracy. Finally, they need to be able to clearly organize the information they gather.

People need to be comfortable with and proficient at consulting diverse sources and asking questions to find the most useful and current knowledge. The goal is to discover better ways to perform a task or complete a job. According to Carter Cast, former CEO of Walmart, "Learning agility may be the most important trait of them all. . . . That trait drives creativity and leads to innovation."[5]

The underlying reason is the rapid increase in the power of digital technology. The ability to curate information will become increasingly important as an ever-increasing amount of information needs to be read, reviewed, analyzed, sorted, and organized into usable chunks. Managers and learners must co-create and co-curate knowledge. Anything learners want to know is at their fingertips, but people need to work together to make sense of this information, determine what is accurate and useful, and apply it to their work. The day of a single person or even a group of people functioning as the expert is gone. The group mind is the new expert.

Critical Thinking

Critical thinking skills were not in great demand during the last economic paradigm, when the focus was on people's hands and their skill and talent using those hands. In a managing minds world, however, thinking, especially the ability to think about things that are complex, is essential. It is viewed as one of the higher-order thinking skills and is not something that people are born with—critical thinking ability is learned and practiced.

This skill enables people to acquire new knowledge that is aligned with the goals of the organization, and to find ways to apply it on the job. Critical thinking skills are the ability to take risks and think outside the box. You need to carefully analyze, synthesize, and consider a response to challenging situations. In other words, you need to be able to think independently, clearly, and rationally about what to believe and do.

Effective Communication

At the heart of all interpersonal skills is communication, and effective communication requires the ability to:

- Be mindful of yourself.
- Listen closely to others to understand, not to convince.
- Withhold judgment.
- Ask open-ended questions.
- Express ideas clearly both nonverbally and verbally.
- Use a variety of technology tools and communication channels as appropriate.

People with these skills are capable of active listening. They first strive to understand before they are understood. They have the ability to ask relevant questions and provide useful feedback. They also have the social skills needed to interact easily with others. These skills form the basis of effective communication, enabling people to learn from others and share what they know, which is essential to a company that is managing minds.

Active Participation

A company managing minds depends on everyone proactively sharing what they are learning. It should build a process for evaluating and measuring how proactively sharing learning has improved performance and helped achieve other organizational goals. The organization needs to communicate to all its members that they are now responsible for their own learning, and therefore must be active participants in that learning. But, it should also demonstrate its commitment to employees by providing what they need to be active participants, such as time to learn, communicate, and collaborate, and making sure the necessary tools and technology are in place.

Managers should communicate clearly that they are asking all employees to actively seek out the information they need to improve their skills, request help if needed, and put what they have learned into practice on the job. They should also share their understanding that learning is a process that occurs over time, rather than in one class or seminar.

Self-Reflection

People need to be able to absorb and examine what they have learned. The reason is simple and basic to the process of learning: We reflect by internally reviewing what we are seeing, hearing, and doing, and learn as a result of this reflection. Honest self-reflection requires the use of many of the other skills necessary for investigation, critical thinking, creativity, and openness. Of all the skills a self-directed learner can possess, self-reflection is the most difficult to attain and one of the most important to maintain.

Self-reflection starts by asking yourself a few pointed questions about an activity, and asking your direct reports to do the same. These questions are:

- What did I want to have happen?
- What did I observe?
- How did I contribute to the results (positive and negative)?
- What could I have done to achieve better results?
- What have I learned from this experience?

Then discuss your answers with others on your team. This will set an example for the people you manage and contribute to an environment that supports learning.

Creativity

Creativity in an organization is not about creating works of art. The focus in this context is on finding new ways to get something done, making something happen, or finding a new idea that proves to be valuable and useful. It can mean the ability to search for solutions, answers, ideas, or strategies. A company cannot successfully manage minds unless it encourages, develops, and rewards creativity that leads to innovation, that is, new ideas and alternative ways of solving problems and challenges.

In his book, *A Whole New Mind: Why Right-Brainers Will Rule the Future*, Daniel Pink says it most succinctly: "Creativity gives you a competitive advantage by adding value to your service or product, and differentiating your business from the competition."[6] In the current, highly competitive environment, companies need creative employees and managers who encourage and reward this behavior.

Emotional Intelligence

A managing minds company needs to be open to the ideas of people who are new to the organization, come from different cultures and backgrounds, and have had different experiences. People in a managing minds organization need to show this openness to one another at all levels of the company. Everyone in the company needs to be open to new ideas, even if they are startlingly different from their current beliefs.

These skills are part of a person's emotional intelligence quotient (EQ). In a company managing minds, employees' EQ is more important than their IQ. Traditionally, IQ has been known as the hard skills factor in the success of people who are managing hands: A high IQ often resulted in being hired, getting raises, moving up the corporate ladder, and generally advancing your career. EQ was always considered a soft skill that was not as valuable. But as companies became more focused on managing the whole person, soft skills have been elevated to equal status. It has been reported that of the skills most needed by people in 2020, EQ tops the list.[7]

High EQ is a prerequisite to professional success in a company in which communication and collaboration are critical. It includes the ability and maturity to:

- Empathize with others.
- Acknowledge, control, and express your emotions.
- Read and assess others' emotions.
- Understand emotional meanings and use emotions to facilitate communication.

Managers in an organization managing minds must learn to develop their own and their employees' EQ to be successful.

Communities of Learners and Practice

Continuous learning happens best in a community of learners, and creating that community requires current communication tools such as email and instant messaging, as well as face-to-face gatherings. These communities comprise employees who share the same learning need.

In communities of learners, employees are networked together as they participate in a learning solution. They may be in the same training or e-learning program, have the same mentor, be part of the same action learning experience, or have a deep interest in the same topic. The community forms a cohort that studies and learns together.

Here is a list of guidelines for people in a learning community:

- There is no such thing as a stupid question.
- Be aware of your cohorts' time zones.
- Keep your cohort in the loop when you will not be available.
- If you do not know, the only acceptable answer is "I don't know."
- Post your questions and answers for everyone to see.
- Stay on topic; information must be related to the subject of common interest.
- Don't waste time on anything not related to the subject of common interest.

The advantages of people learning and working together are significant. Questions can be answered anytime by communicating with the cohort. The cohort also brings different levels of knowledge and experience. With enough trust, peers are willing to open up about work problems and issues that they might not want to discuss with a manager. And some learning is best done in a social context.

When that community of learners graduates, it evolves and can become part of a worldwide, always-on community of practice. This ensures that learning continues. Get enough people connected in that community of practice and you will find that the community has encountered almost every problem, dealt with any imaginable issue, uncovered all the questions, and most likely answered the ones that are critical. It's not exactly *The Matrix* head jack, but it's as close as today's technology comes.

A community of practice is another platform for social learning, and a concept first discussed in *Communities of Practice* in 1998 by Etienne Wegner.[8] It was a managing minds idea that was born in a managing hands world. The community of practice has three main characteristics:

1. **Domain:** It has a shared area of interest that members are committed to learning about.

2. **Practice:** Members of the community use what they learn and practice what they know and know how to do.

3. **Community:** Members also work with other people to compile hints, experiences, stories, and solutions.

Learners can connect to the community of practice with any device, anytime and anywhere. They can read the answer to their question, listen to the answer, watch a video of the answer, or look at a schematic for the answer. They can follow an answer step by step if they have a process or procedure question. They can even snap a photo and show the work they did to the people who are telling them what to do, so they can make sure that the red wire goes where the red wire needs to go. Learning—getting the answer now—is an extension of the experience of learning taken away from the community of learners. If they want to learn something more, they have to learn to ask the right questions, find the person with the answers, and seek answers in the right community.

The idea of one company prohibiting employees from sharing knowledge with another is a vestige of the old managing hands "knowledge is power" mindset. It's impossible to control the flow of knowledge in a world where people can communicate from anywhere and anytime, so the old restrictions on what people can learn are disappearing. With a managing minds mindset, using communities of learners and practice to your advantage produces greater performance gains, faster time to performance, increased agility, better solutions, and a higher corporate IQ.

Consider this example from Xerox, which has more than 25,000 field service technicians worldwide. They are all part of a growing community of practice called Eureka. When a field service tech comes up with a great idea, a new solution, or even a good tip for a repair, it goes into Eureka. Every day, in every part of the world, field service techs come up with good ideas in the course of doing their jobs. Even though Xerox tied the results to money, the real incentive for participation was recognition by their peers. Being a well-respected Eureka thought leader able to solve difficult problems drives people to learn, find better ways of doing something, solve problems, and share that knowledge. The results translate into millions of dollars saved each year in more effective service calls, as well as greater customer satisfaction.[9]

Imagine the benefits of a really large, widespread community of people who do the same thing, only for different companies. In a managing minds world, they would be collaborating and communicating to one another's benefit, and the customers would be the winners.

Learning From Failure and Success

Before we look at the way failure should be viewed in a managing minds company, let's distinguish between real learning and rote learning. At the heart of managing minds is what we call real learning, which is diametrically opposite to rote learning. It is important to understand how they are different.

Real learning is uninhibited learning. It's freeform, creative, messy, unconstrained, and improvisational You learn by continuously exploring, inventing, failing, and then succeeding. Failing is hardwired into the process of real learning. Real learning—the kind of aha moment signaling that the brain has connected the dots—is a wonderful and amazing mystery. It involves long-term memory, synapses, endorphins, and encoding. Real learning is a result of those accidental and serendipitous moments. That's what we mean by uninhibited.

Rote learning is inhibited, by-the-book learning. It's bound by rules, guidelines, regulations, procedures, facts, and figures. It is designed to be shunted into short-term memory, regurgitated quickly, measured against the right answers, and just as quickly forgotten. Rote learning is too often the way training is presented, and one of the primary reasons people do not remember and therefore do not learn.

There's a science to real learning that is often overlooked. Every time—and we mean every time—you learn to do something new, you have done so by trial and error. Genius short-circuits the process. Talent gets you there quicker, but the process of learning is the same: trial and error. The latest neuroscience findings show us that the brain aggregates memory and builds trial and error into the way to do something. It appears that the "failed" trial and error cells are held back, while the "successful" trial and no error cells are moved to the front of the line. The current theory is that the old trial and error cells get recycled.[10]

It is imperative in a managing minds company that real learning is enabled and not disabled. The fear of failure is the most powerful disabler of real learning. The fear actually has a name: atychiphobia. While that phobia is a debilitating anxiety with serious mental and physical repercussions, many of us are reluctant to take risks that might result in what we perceive to be a loss of respect, status, or career. We also worry about spending time and money on something that doesn't succeed, but those are only proxies for self-esteem. The problem is that without risk taking and the failures that inevitably come with that, learning is limited and nothing truly new and innovative is created.

So fear disables the trial and error process from Pre-K onward. In a managing hands environment, you have an entire workforce of people who do not try anything new or different because they are afraid to fail. They do not innovate, create, or disrupt, and move from trial and error to tried and true. There is only rote learning to fall back on, with all its limitations. You will never in today's world of change and surprises be able to learn everything you need to know and do in every situation.

A quick story to make a point: Thomas Edison was interviewed after he got the first light bulb to work (that is, stay lighted for more than a minute), and was asked, "How did you manage to keep trying since you tried and failed over 1,000 times to get it right?" He told the reporter, "Those 1,000 times it didn't work were all lessons that got me that much closer to the one that works." Therefore, a managing minds organization does not punish risk takers, but rather embraces every failure as part of the learning process that leads to success. If Edison's work was an equation, it would be Risk × Failure × 1,000 = Success.

As we learned from Edison, innovation often requires failure before success. If we truly want innovation, we need to make room for failure. Failure results in new ways of getting from here to there. And that's essentially at the heart innovation. If innovation requires real learning, and managing minds requires real learning, then innovation requires managing minds.

We have mentioned failure throughout this book, and in organizations still held captive by the managing hands mentality, failing is something to be avoided at all costs. It's a problem to be punished.

Failure at any point along a production line means the line stops and production halts. Worse is if the failure slips through and reaches the customer, because then the company's reputation suffers. But we are moving away from managing hands and need to change the way we think about failure.

In a company that is managing minds, when the final product or service is not irrevocable or irreversible and is continuously evolving and improving, failure shouldn't be a punishable offense. A company successfully managing minds must accept that failures are a critical element in learning. This does not mean that managers need to overlook mistakes and praise and reward those people who consistently fail. It means that a company that desires to manage minds and wants to add pull learning to their push training must embrace failure as a great opportunity to learn and grow. To begin that evolution of thinking about failure, it is important to first understand the different roles that failure plays in the process of learning.

Failures, like successes, exist on a continuum from the unavoidable to the unexplored, from the minor to the major, from the disruptive to the disastrous. We have three categories in which we place failures and ways to take advantage of each:

- unavoidable failures
- unanticipated failures
- anticipated failures.

Unavoidable Failures

As we already highlighted, push training is delivered out of context, usually too early to be needed, with little or no opportunity for application of what is learned, and zero follow-up. It is a recipe for failure. Learners are left on their own to recall what to do. And when they forget, which they inevitably will, they interrupt someone else to ask a question, ask Siri or Alexa, or try to Google the answer. Even worse, when they forget and are afraid of appearing stupid, they might take their best guess or simply not do anything, which is when failures occur. These are the unavoidable failures that happen when people forget what they have learned despite the training they received.

These failures can be avoided by using many of the ideas about extended training we already mentioned. Instead of only providing the training program, include pre- and post-training as well. Pre-training might have people reading material the course will cover or watching a video of the process or procedure they will learn. Even if the material is used in the classroom, skimming or watching it beforehand can make a difference in the level of retention.

The goal is to make the training more compelling, memorable, interactive, relevant, and most of all, applicable. Learning takes time. The parts of our brain that own the learning process require time, reinforcement, experimentation, failure, relearning, and repetition. Training starts in the classroom or online and continues back on the job until the new knowledge and know-how really stick. Adding a performance support tool—from experts available on social media to an on-the-job accessible knowledge repository—will enable remembering and defeat forgetting. Unavoidable failures are almost always traceable to forgetting the actual task or procedural steps, or being distracted and not paying attention.

Add up the cost of the unavoidable failures and weigh it against the cost of the extended training. In manufacturing companies alone, the cost of failure in 2015 was estimated at between 20 and 30 percent of the total cost of sales.[11]

No one has managed to provide an overall number for the cost of failure across industries and companies in any given year. However, we can assume that the total cost of unavoidable failures is staggering. Learning from failure is always cheaper than the cost of repairs, mistakes, lost time, downtime, injuries, accidents, and breakdowns.

Unanticipated Failures

Even when you have done a good job of real learning, unanticipated failures happen. These failures occur in the process of adapting what you learn when you encounter a situation that is so unusual, unique, or unpredictable that the response needed is not part of your ability to react. They occur in workplaces in which there are many parts— equipment, machines, or people—that are interconnected, complex, and interdependent.

These failures happen in the course of working in relatively complex jobs where the unexpected often happens and triggers a series of failures. The Three Mile Island meltdown started with a candle. Inspectors forgot to replace a small safety valve on the Piper Bravo oil rig, causing an explosion that killed 167 workers. A booster joint with weak sealant failed in freezing temperatures, causing the space shuttle *Challenger* explosion. The list goes on. These are the failures that resulted in the most costly lessons. They were not anticipated, but they all started with small failures that compounded. The big lesson is to rapidly identify and fix small failures before they become unmanageable. And that takes us back to providing extended training and continuous learning in the workplace that supports remembering and making the right decisions, especially in stressful situations.

Anticipated Failures

Finally, anticipated failures are the ones we want. They lead to new products, discoveries, and inventions that push a company past the competition. Anticipated failures drive amazing leaps forward in our understanding of the way the universe works. Failure happens. But it presents the opportunity for a learning experience.

Anticipated failures happen because we want to experiment, to discover answers to questions, to confront the unknown, to simply see what happens when we try something new. Anticipated failures produce exciting and new and innovative products and services. There is nothing in our world today that we use—from the light bulbs that help us see to the food we eat to the airplanes in which we travel—that was not a result of some anticipated failure that ultimately led to success. These failures are the ones worth investing in, whether they happen serendipitously or are part of a longer, larger-scale R&D effort.

In companies managing minds, experimentation and failure are part of the path that leads to innovation and success. Failure is valued and enabled and supported. Amazon and Netflix are great examples of managing minds companies unafraid to test the waters. Some experiments work; others not so much. In a company managing minds, the alternative is fear of failing, which leads to the dull, unimpressive stagnation that precedes the loss of the best minds and is a marker for a slow company death.

The real failure is the failure to redefine failure as an important part of the process of managing minds. Only strong leadership can redefine failure and make it OK for people to fail. Everyone in the company needs to follow that lead. Failures of any type need to be reviewed, not as part of the blame game, but to ask, "What happened, why did it happen, and what can we learn?" The code of silence where everyone is afraid to report or take responsibility for a failure is part of a managing hands world. The idea of failing and keeping it quiet until it is inherited by whoever takes your job is a short-term fix that will not work in the long term. Failures need to be seen as an opportunity for learning.

This type of new thinking about failure can be seen in all the companies we researched and many others that are managing minds. All learning and information is good input going forward to make a company and its culture, products, and services better. And it translates into more value for its customers.

6

POLICIES AND WORKSPACES

In the previous industrial economy of managing hands, work was all about what you did. If you could do it faster and cheaper legally (but not necessarily ethically), it was business as usual. If you closed the lid on your moral compass when it no longer seemed useful, that was OK. You could have the illusion that you were invisible and focus solely on doing the "next thing right."[1]

There are too many notorious examples of companies that have failed to do what is right: The BP Deepwater Horizon explosion. GM's faulty ignition switches. Takata airbag ruptures. Volkswagen emissions fraud. Simplicity crib deaths. Samsung phone fires. Wells Fargo customer deception. This partial list is itself a sad indictment of the focus on maximizing profits. In each case, it was eventually discovered that people within the company knew about ethical violations, but the company culture discouraged those individuals from speaking up. What's worse is that the company's management was motivated to proceed even though the risk of failure and criminal negligence was high.

Those were some of the headline-grabbing breaches of ethics. Many more unreported yet still unethical actions occur every day in the workplace: deciding to pad travel expenses, passing on confidential company information, spinning data to make company performance look better, accepting kickbacks to complete a business deal, undermining a co-worker to pass that person for promotion. And then there are the daily personal ways we act unethically, such as removing something from someone else's desk without permission or taking credit for someone else's work. These are reflections of an organizational culture focused on secrecy, lack of empathy, dishonesty, and fear, all of which hinder a company trying to get the best from people.

Doing What's Right

In today's world, where you, your employees, and your company are completely transparent, your reputation is your most valuable asset. Everything you do is visible, and being invisible is no longer an option. Now it's all about how you operate. The things that you produce can be made by almost anyone. Who you are is unique. According to Dov Seidman, founder of LRN, an ethics and compliance management firm, "We're no longer asking everybody to do the next thing right; but to do the next right thing."[2]

Companies that are learning to manage minds are focused on being open, transparent organizations in which collaboration and communication are basic operating principles. They believe that sharing knowledge is power, and continuous learning is the key to successfully meeting the challenges of the knowledge economy. Failures are to be learned from and not hidden. Opposing viewpoints and ideas are valued and listened to by everyone in the company. Conversations are open and honest. The hierarchy of roles, and the secrecy and compartmentalization that go with it, has been replaced by the hierarchy of ideas, in which openness is a prerequisite.

By comparison, companies that are managing hands are cultures in which playing follow the leader is serious business and means not asking for justification of decisions. These companies support behaviors ranging from not daring to ask questions or disagreeing with management to not thinking for yourself. Blindly obeying the rules, being nice and agreeable, and showing that you are successful at any cost are considered the norm.

A company driven by collaboration, cooperation, and communication instead of command and control means people must be open and honest with one another. They must be able to trust that their co-workers and managers are telling the truth. Worldblu, an organization that has spent more than a decade of research on organizational democracy, has identified integrity as one of its 10 key principles of success. For them, a successful organization in today's economy depends on "doing what is morally and ethically right."[3]

Trust is the cornerstone of learning. If I do not trust you, I won't learn from you. If I don't trust my company, I will not be engaged enough to learn and develop my abilities on behalf of that organization. An organization without ethics is an organization in which no one can be trusted. And an organization devoid of trust is an organization that cannot learn and grow and change. When you manage hands, trust is not important. People are considered cogs on the wheel and can easily be replaced. When you manage minds, people are your greatest asset. Their ability to grow and learn is the key to your success.

Managing minds companies know it's smart business to make ethics a priority. It's that simple. And companies that are managing minds are invested in enabling smart people to make the right decisions. The most visible way in which that support can be demonstrated is to have managers set the example. When managers condone behavior that crosses the line, employees will interpret that as permission to behave unethically. If managers are not honest in reporting the performance of their teams, team members will not see the point of turning in their best performance.

Managers need to support people who are doing the right thing. We're not talking about giving lip service to ethics by listing this value on a lunchroom poster or HR memo. We're talking about working ethically every minute of every day. We need principled leadership from managers focused on doing the right thing. We need managers who convey this value to the people with whom they work, and have it be the standard in everything they do.

According to John Baldoni, in his book *The Leader's Pocket Guide: 101 Indispensable Tools, Tips, and Techniques for Any Situation*, to head off unethical behavior, leaders should "be seen, be heard, and be there."[4] This means adhering to a very specific set of actions, many of which would be familiar to a manager in a company managing minds:

Be seen:
- Visit people where they work.
- Use teleconferences to stay in touch visually with your teams.
- Institute an open-door policy so people can visit you if they need to.
- Hold meetings where the work is done: in the cube, on the shop floor, and so on.

Be heard:
- Deliver consistent messages. Make your messages clear, coherent, and concise.
- Listen more than you speak.
- Check for understanding.
- Invite feedback from your direct reports and colleagues.

Be there:
- Always be accessible and available to help.
- Lead by example.
- Act for the good of the team.
- If sacrifice is required, be the first to volunteer.

Baldoni writes that when a crisis does arise due to the company or individuals breaking the rules, managers need to step up and quickly address the wrongs by confronting the problem and coming clean, fixing the problem with the interests of the person or people who were wronged in mind, listening to their complaints, apologizing and making restitution, and staying engaged until the problem is resolved. This course of action is not easy, especially when people have been harmed by something the company did, but it is the right thing to do, and the only way to head off disaster for your organization.[5]

It's impossible to anticipate and simulate every ethical dilemma that people might face in the course of their workday. The ambiguity of each situation is not something you can prepare for in a course or program. Managers must help people learn to make the right choices for the business. This means learning how to be clear about a situation, understanding the ethical dilemma, identifying the consequences of the wrong choice, and choosing to make the right decision. It goes beyond showing people what to do. Being clear about the situation, understanding the consequences, and making the right choices can only be learned on the job. It is a continuous learning process in which what you have learned to do is continually being adopted and adapted in a constantly changing set of circumstances and new environments.

A managing minds company cares about people and about learning, open and honest communication and collaboration, trust and honesty, and doing the "next right thing" instead of only doing the next thing more quickly, cheaply, or profitably. You do not need to be managing minds to be an ethical company, but it helps.

Rethinking the Employee Handbook

When trying to embed an ethical culture that does what's right, it's important to start with the employee handbook and the onboarding process. And yet, this policy guidebook should not be dedicated just to compliance; it should a signal to current and prospective employees that you mean business. Managing minds companies set the expectation for continuous learning from day one. Let's look at some ideas for bringing along employees who have just been hired.

In a managing hands company, the employee handbook, often a retread from the previous year and handed out as a standard part of the first few days on the job, is most useful as a sleep aid. The information is the playbook for the defense, written by a committee of people who remember every problem, infraction, broken rule, and violated HR policy and are attempting to cover themselves so they don't have to call the legal department. It's an encyclopedia of problems that no one in the company ever wants to have happen again. A better name would be *The You Are a Liability Handbook*. Even worse, it is an artifact of a bureaucratic world of managing hands, flooded with paperwork and documentation, that tries to avoid individual accountability and responsibility, and acts to inhibit—if not actually prohibit—individual initiative. It's the exact opposite of what you are trying to accomplish in a managing minds environment.

In a company that is managing minds, the employee handbook should be a page-turner filled with excitement and encouragement for new people looking forward to working in the company. They want to know that they will be working with a great team—a company filled with people who communicate and collaborate, share decisions, have an open dialogue, can be creative, grow professionally and personally, are recognized for their contributions, and play and succeed together.

The employee handbook is more important than you imagine. It's a guidebook of your managing minds company, an introduction to how employees are expected to act in what is probably a very different culture than any they have ever encountered. Your company is a foreign country, and the employee handbook is the equivalent of a *Lonely Planet* travel guide.

An employee handbook for a managing minds organization should capture the vision you want people to have as they work for you. It is the first time all the employees get a chance to really find out what they have gotten themselves into, and it may well be the only piece of information that everyone is required to read. It's true: You only get one chance to make a great first impression.

Most of the people you hire have been forced to wade through an employee handbook before. The mere words *employee handbook* probably make them tune out immediately, while they wait for the chance to get to work. So first, give it an attention-grabbing name; you want to call it something that is compelling. Here are some examples to kick-start your imagination:

- *The Sterling Culture Code* (Sterling Mining Company)
- *A Voyage to Pluto* (Memória Visual)
- *Reference Guide on Our Freedom and Responsibility Culture* (Netflix)
- *Welcome to ZGM* (ZGM)

- *The Next Chapter* (Zappos)
- *Culture Code: Creating a Lovable Company* (HubSpot).

And while a title may be interesting and catchy, the way it looks counts even more. You are marketing and selling the company and the idea that you are managing minds. Make it beautiful. Have it look so inviting that people want to see what's inside. Design it for use online, and make it interactive and available on mobile devices whenever an employee needs to find an answer.

Zappos made *The Next Chapter* like a comic book, full of pictures, drawings, and short stories of the great experiences people have working there. Netflix created a great presentation. Memória Visual produced *Voyage to Pluto* to read like a graphic novel. It's your chance to show employees that they are valued and important. You want to start to engage their minds.

New employees want to know what they can expect from your company, not only professionally but personally. With lots of choices about where to work, they picked your company, and this is a great opportunity to remind them why they did. Put the perks up front. Here are some real examples from top managing minds companies:

- gourmet cafeterias
- employee lounges
- access to professional development
- tuition reimbursement
- company carpools and buses
- on-site daycare
- gyms and personal trainers
- equal same-sex and opposite-sex benefits
- maternity and paternity leave
- eldercare time off
- mental health days.

If you think this list is for the high-tech elite, guess again. It's taken from a wide sampling of some of the top managing minds companies across a variety of industries out there today.[6]

Until managing minds is the rule in workplaces worldwide, people will be in transition from the managing hands approach. So it's important to clearly tell people about the vision and mission of the company and remind them why they must bring their minds to work every day.

In words and pictures, employee stories, posters and bumper stickers, make sure people are reminded about continuous learning. Show them examples of successful failures your company has experienced. Point out that the command-and-control method they are so used to has been replaced by communicate and collaborate. Illustrate how sharing knowledge is power. Highlight stories about the importance of a growth mindset. The point is to bring to the forefront how great it will be to work in a company that is firmly planted in the 21st century.

Only 20 percent of employees working in a traditional organization can recite its values, understand why they are important, or know how to incorporate them into their daily work.[7] In contrast, at UKTV, the United Kingdom's biggest multichannel broadcasting company, more than 90 percent of its employees can not only name the values—create, learn, influence, challenge, and collaborate—but also explain how the values guide them in their daily work, because those values are actively promoted. Posters bearing these values decorate the office walls and several initiatives further encourage UKTV staff to implement these values.[8]

Employees are smart enough to know that there are rules that need to be followed. We have all gone to employee indoctrinations, where an entire morning was taken up by someone from security telling us all the ways we could be fired. Employees get it and do not need to hear it—or read it—more than once. Besides, you want to begin building a culture of trust, and there is no better way to do that than to communicate your trust of employees from the day they walk in the door.

This is your opportunity to separate your company from the rest with an engaging and honest employee-centric guide to your company. It is the traveler's guide to one of the most interesting places to work. You can minimize risk and use this as an opportunity to build an exciting culture at the same time. The goal is to have the handbook be so well received that it is used as a recruiting tool to entice the best minds to work for you. After all, in a managing minds world, the best minds are the ones you want.

Revamping the Workspace

After new employees finish reading the exciting guide to your company, they need to get to work. If they are not working from home, a coffee shop, or some virtual space, they will need to come to the office. Will your office reflect a managing minds ideal, or will it be a typical 20th-century cube farm, designed to control behavior, not facilitate learning and performance?

"Form follows function" in a managing minds environment. If we want communication and collaboration for continuous learning, then we need to design spaces that support this behavior. The knowledge economy is all about thinking, writing, meeting, sharing, researching, creating, innovating, and designing. The best managing minds companies have already started to discover how to create a physical environment that enables that work.[9]

People need to be able to choose where to work without the old hierarchy getting in the way. Offices should have a variety of spaces in which to work alone, in small groups, or larger gatherings. All of these spaces should be comfortable and inviting. They should allow people to work standing, sitting, walking, reclining, or huddling together—whatever works for them needs to be available.

The technology should help people communicate and collaborate as well. This can be as simple as having access to cloud storage, computer screens, Wi-Fi and cellphone connectivity, walls that function as whiteboard space, digital whiteboards, and videoconferencing technology.

People also need ways to express who they are and make a statement about their identity. Personal spaces should be filled with whatever creative stuff people want to display, not cookie-cutter offices devoid of anything that makes it feel as if they belong to nobody in particular. In a managing hands environment, people were replaceable; one pair of hands could be swapped out for another. In a managing minds space, everyone is an individual, and every mind is special.

In the industrial economy, the predominant color was gray, the color of concrete and steel. In a modern managing minds environment, people need more variation. Warm colors and shapes, striking forms and patterns, different textures and materials, even water and plants—all of it is part of the enticing, interesting, colorful workscape that helps people do the work their minds are being asked to do.

Finally, people need private spaces where they can retreat to think or not think. Provide spaces that support the work while also offering havens where people can recharge and renew their energy. Provide spaces where phone calls and meetings will not disturb others.

Steelcase, one of the oldest and most respected providers of office furniture, is one of the design companies leading the way to this new type of working environment. Its "Resilient Workplace" is no comparison to the old cube farm that is still so ubiquitous. The company has created an Innovation Center and WorkCafé to test ideas about workspaces that provide greater well-being, offer more interaction balanced by the need for privacy, establish areas for specific needs such as videoconferencing, and give employees working in a managing minds organization what they need to be as productive as possible.[10]

Similarly, Menlo Innovations does a variation on the open-office design, with everyone working together around tables in the middle of a large undivided space. The purpose of the Menlo workspace is to facilitate teamwork, information sharing, and problem solving to develop the best software solutions for their customers. Prospective new hires are given some time to try out this environment before they are hired. The company knows that its workspace design is not a good fit for everyone and some people walk away after deciding that they don't want to work in that kind of environment. Those who have stayed have created a very positive and productive working culture.[11]

All the best managing minds companies we looked at use space to their advantage. By freeing your employees to work in places that they'll actually enjoy, you can start to build a company that reflects your belief in managing minds.

7

MAKING THE SHIFT

It should be clear by now that organizations everywhere need to stop managing hands and transition to managing minds to succeed in the knowledge economy. This chapter will show you how to make the shift.

People in a company fall along a continuum from protectors to innovators.[1] Protectors do exactly what the term implies; they protect the status quo. They are too uncomfortable with the idea of change to try anything new and different. Their goal is to make sure things stay the same so that nothing they have—titles, power, prestige, salary, perks, and so on—is lost. They fall into the "that's the way we always do it!" camp.

The innovators, on the other hand, are the people who like to be challenged by a new and potentially better way of doing things. They are strongly motivated by the idea that the "new" can get them more— work-life balance, time to think, personal time, recognition, purpose, autonomy, safety, and meaning—from work. The key is to learn how to work with everyone along the continuum.

Start selling the idea of managing minds and converting the protectors rather than gathering the forces of the innovators, who are already believers and willing to try a new approach. Find out what the protectors are afraid of and what they fear they will lose. Once you have listened to them and heard what they are feeling, begin the process of showing them that the real risk is not changing. Provide evidence that doing things the way they always have leads to stagnation and loss of the ability to compete, innovate, be agile, make better decisions, provide a better workplace for everyone, and ultimately make the company more successful in the knowledge economy. Use the companies described in this book as real-world examples of why managing minds is a better approach than managing hands. If there are examples of managing minds in your organization, highlight them.[2]

Once the protectors have begun to accept the idea, you can bring the innovators into the circle. But even with the innovators, you need to make a solid case. They may be predisposed to the new idea and to going along with the changes, but they aren't automatons. Sell them as well. Listen to what they hope to gain. Prove that managing minds can help them realize their vision. The innovators, once sold, become your champions, adding their own thoughts and ideas to support the reasons why managing minds is the best way to manage a company. Be sure everyone recognizes their contributions. Let them become missionaries for the idea and spread it into the organization in their own voice.[3]

When you have won over both groups, you can present the idea of working in a managing minds organization as a shared vision. There will still be arguments and disagreements about how to make it happen, but that's a very different discussion from why it should be done.

You cannot manage minds unless the company is totally focused on learning. Its values, beliefs, and work environment must make learning the top priority. We both have seen people return from a training program, conference, or webinar with the excitement of having learned something new. What they learned might have been a new sales technique, software program, or a machine that has the potential to increase performance. In companies that do not embrace and support continuous learning, the reaction is too often about dismissing what they learned, either in word or deed. The investment of time and energy is never returned, because what was learned was never adopted, adapted, and applied.

Creating the Right Culture

The culture that underpins a managing minds approach must support and encourage an ongoing and collective discovery, sharing, and application of knowledge and skills at the individual, team, and organization levels. A culture that supports managing minds is a culture of inquiry; an environment in which people feel safe challenging the status quo, taking risks, and enhancing the quality of what they do for customers, themselves, shareholders, and other stakeholders. A company managing minds maintains a culture in which learning how to learn is valued and accepted, and the pursuit of learning is woven into the fabric of organizational life.

So how do you really know if you have a company that is managing minds? What are the visible signs? What are the metrics? How do you know if your organization has the DNA that predisposes it to learning? Gary Neilson and Jaime Estupiñán have been studying and writing about organizational DNA for the past 10 years. They explain it this way: "We use the term *organizational DNA* as a metaphor for the underlying organizational and cultural design factors that define an organization's personality and determine whether it is strong or weak in executing strategy."[4]

Using this DNA metaphor, here are 10 principles that determine whether a company is doing what needs to be done to promote and support managing minds. When people behave according to these principles, the enterprise is predisposed to learning at all levels. The conditions exist to be able to manage minds, not just hands. As you review the items, ask yourself if you are enabling or disabling these principles:

1. **Leaders support learning.** The message from the CEO, senior executives, and other key thought leaders in the organization is that continuous learning by individuals, teams, and the organization is not only valued but expected. Leaders communicate that learning can happen in many different ways: face-to-face and online instruction, push training and pull learning, on-the-job activities, and social interaction. Leaders say and do things that are visibly aligned with this value.

2. **Managers take responsibility for managing minds.**
   Managers encourage their direct reports to acquire new
   knowledge and skills and develop competencies that make
   them more valuable to the organization. They provide
   opportunities to learn, adopt, adapt, practice, and apply what
   their employees learned on the job. Managers hold people
   accountable for learning, and take responsibility for ensuring
   the growth and development of the people they manage.

3. **The organization hires and promotes learners.** Recruiters,
   other HR staff, and hiring managers ask questions about
   what applicants have recently learned and look for people
   who are self-motivated learners. These individuals are
   always seeking opportunities to acquire new knowledge
   and skills, learn from their successes and failures, take
   risks for the purpose of learning, and continue to develop
   themselves. The organization selects new hires and
   promotes current employees who demonstrate initiative in
   learning and growing.

4. **Learning is aligned with results.** Managers can clearly
   explain how acquiring specific knowledge and skills will
   contribute to the success of the organization. It's not learning
   for learning's sake, or learning because "we've always done
   it that way," but learning because that's what will help the
   company achieve its strategic goals.

5. **People have a growth mindset.** Executives, managers, and
   employees believe that they and others can learn and grow
   within the organization. They believe that this potential is
   in everyone and can be unleashed by actively giving people
   the opportunity to acquire new knowledge and skills.
   They believe that nobody is fixed in their abilities, that it
   is human nature to want to enhance competencies and
   improve performance.

6. **Organizational structure facilitates learning.** Information
   flows freely throughout the organization. Leaders of work
   units don't hesitate to communicate with one another, and

they provide assistance and peer coaching as needed. People are connected across departments and geography and actively share successes, failures, and lessons learned. Other key stakeholders are brought into important decision-making situations and are respected for their input. Change can be a result of a top-down or bottom-up initiative.

7. **Knowledge management contributes to learning.** Information is stored in an easily accessible place (hardcopy or in an LMS database) that can be accessed and used by people to acquire the knowledge they need to be successful in their work. Successes and failures are equally and openly described so people can learn from them. People are constantly creating, identifying, collecting, organizing, sharing, adopting, adapting, and using information to help the company become smarter.

8. **People take risks and experiment.** Managers foster this behavior by recognizing the effort and new insights even if the results are unsatisfactory. People are not punished for trying something new. On the contrary, risk taking in the name of doing a better job is encouraged. Failures, as well as successes, are treated as opportunities for learning. People are fearless.

9. **Learning is rewarded.** Individuals are recognized and applauded for acquiring new knowledge and skills. When new learning is applied and contributes to improving the performance of the organization, people are rewarded. This reward is not necessarily monetary. What's important is that the reward is appreciated and reinforces this kind of behavior.

10. **Everyone is reflective.** Everyone takes every opportunity to learn. Projects end with an after-action review. Client contacts are immediately examined with the intention of learning and improving those contacts in the future. Tasks, events, processes, and committees are all viewed as opportunities for learning from the past. Everyone actively participates in communities of learning and graduates to be

involved in communities of practice. People are continually reflecting on what they can learn from what they are doing, what they did well, what could be done better, what was accomplished, and how it made the company a smarter organization. There are no giant egos that need to be the final arbiter for all important decisions and, regardless of outcomes or reality, must always be right, blaming everyone else for any failures. In a reflective environment, no one is ever thrown under the bus.

In a managing minds culture, these 10 principles are apparent in the stated values of the organization, and those stated values are aligned with the values in use. In other words, these values are not only written and spoken, but also evident in employees' day-to-day behavior.

Here are some examples of alignment and misalignment of managing minds values:

The stated value is, "We want all employees to develop their skills and abilities."

An executive assistant asks her boss for permission to attend a series of workshops on financial management that is being offered by the company. She explains that this would help her understand the company better, be more helpful to him, and strengthen her career portfolio. Is the executive's first reaction to say, "I appreciate your ambition, but I need you here right now. We can look at arranging something in the future. And, besides, I don't have the budget for that." Or, is the executive's first reaction to say, "I appreciate your ambition. That would be useful knowledge for you to have. Thanks for bringing this request to my attention. Let's talk about how we can make that happen as soon as possible." Both reactions are reasonable, but one is indicative of a managing minds culture and the other is not.

The stated value is, "We learn from our mistakes."

A project team member reluctantly admits to the team leader that due to some unforeseen factors their project will not come in on time and within budget. Is the team leader's first reaction to say, "I'm very disappointed in our team. Why weren't these problems anticipated? Why wasn't I told about this sooner?" Or, is the team leader's first reaction to say, "Let's get the team together and review what happened. I want us to learn from this experience so that we can do a better job of reaching our goals in the future." Both reactions are reasonable, but one is indicative of a managing minds culture and the other is not.

The stated value is, "We share information and have open and honest lines of communication."

The R&D department of a company has produced several prototypes of an exciting new product that has the potential to become a blockbuster for the company. Manufacturing helped with the prototype but has not learned enough about it yet to move it into production. The marketing department is telling potential customers about the new product and the sales department is taking orders and promising delivery. Is the CEO's first reaction to say, "We have to fast-track this product with manufacturing so that we can fill orders and keep customers happy." Or, is the CEO's first reaction to say, "Let's get all the department heads together and find out what each of them needs to know from the other to successfully launch this new product." Both reactions are reasonable, but one is indicative of a managing minds culture and the other is not.

The stated value is, "We value creativity and innovation."

An employee had an idea for a new mobile app that seemed very promising, and early feedback from customers indicated it was something they would want. However, after a couple of months, the employee discovered that the app couldn't have the intended functionality without being overly complicated and too expensive for customers. Is the first reaction of the employee's boss to say, "What a waste; two months lost. Next time we have to make sure the product will be successful before we start on it. Now, how am I going to explain this to management?" Or, is the first reaction of the employee's boss to say, "Good effort. What did you learn from trying to build the app? What did you learn about developing new products, about collaboration, and about yourself? Is there anything we could have done to help you achieve your goal?" Both reactions are reasonable, but one is indicative of a managing minds culture and the other is not.

The stated value is, "We want feedback and accountability."

The company's leadership team spent three days in an annual meeting developing a strategic plan for the following year. At the end of the first quarter, a manager asked the vice president of planning why they hadn't used the plan to measure their progress and take stock of what they need to do to achieve their goals. Is the vice president's first reaction to say, "It's been a busy quarter and besides, the main reason we have that meeting each year is to get the leadership team together. The plan is out of date as soon as it is done." Or, is the vice president's first reaction to say, "That's a good point. I'm going to recommend that we get the leadership team back together and talk about what we can learn about ourselves and the company by comparing what we said we would do with what's been accomplished." Both reactions are reasonable, but one is indicative of a managing minds culture and the other is not.

The stated value is, "We develop leaders."

A department manager goes to her director with a complaint that she is not getting best effort from her team. She says that they don't follow through on assignments, they are late for meetings, and they don't communicate important decisions to one another. Is the director's first reaction to say, "You're a leader now. You need to take charge and be a leader in your team. They should be looking to you for direction." Or, is the director's first reaction to say, "It seems like you could benefit from a coach who could help you learn how to be a more effective leader in this team. Let's talk about how a coach could be helpful and what kind of coach we should find for you." Both reactions are reasonable, but one is indicative of a managing minds culture and the other is not.

The stated value is, "We value continuous improvement."

A new salesperson is attending a class in relationship selling at a local college. He goes to his sales manager and asks how he could apply what he is learning to their department's sales strategy. Is the sales manager's first reaction to say, "I doubt we can use what you're learning in this sales organization. The way we've always done sales here is by the numbers. You make a certain number of cold calls. A percentage of those turn into presentations and a percentage of those presentations turn into sales. We don't have time for anything else." Or, is the sales manager's first reaction to say, "Tell me about what you are learning in the class. How do you think it could help our sales organization? Let's come up with a plan for how you could experiment with that approach and then we can determine if it's a good fit with our goals." Both reactions are reasonable, but one is indicative of a managing minds culture and the other is not.

The 5 As for Managing Minds

As a manager in the knowledge economy, focused on managing minds, you are responsible for helping employees learn to continuously improve their performance, the performance of their teams, and the entire organization. The ability to learn is a talent, and like any talent, practice leads to improvement. In a business environment where disruption and surprises are the rule, and innovation and rapid decision making the norm, learning becomes an essential competency. There are five key elements—call them the five *As*—that must be present to ensure that people have this competency and are successful in your organization as learners:[5]

1. **Alignment:** aligning learning with individual, team, and organizational goals
2. **Anticipation:** anticipating learning and success from participation in the learning solution and communicating this expectation
3. **Alliance:** forming a learning alliance between employee and manager
4. **Application:** applying learning to achieving business goals
5. **Accountability:** being measurably accountable for business results.

Alignment

Everyone is motivated to participate in learning solutions when they understand how their participation in that activity will help them be more effective in the organization. In many companies that are managing minds, any learning, either personal or professional, is considered important and in concert with the idea of making continuous learning a habit. While it may not be apparent at first, the assumption is that whatever people learn will at some point yield connections that will positively affect the business. Supporting this idea and showing the alignment between what people learn and how they perform, operate, innovate, and collaborate makes the point that continuous learning is what's important. Aligning that learning with the needs and goals of the business will happen. When it does, it is your job to point out that as people increase their brainpower, the IQ and EQ of the organization improves.

Be explicit about the link between whatever people are learning and results. Use the examples of companies that are supporting learning in every form and show that as learning improves what people know and know how to do, both personally or professionally, these companies are more successful. Although aligning what people are learning to business goals may not always be as apparent as it was when learning was pushed from the company, it does help instill a culture of learning, in which learning is a key factor in the success of the company.

Anticipation

Educators and neuroscientists who study what helps people learn know that anticipation of success is a major factor in learning. The research on expectations is clear: People who expect to increase their knowledge and skills are more likely to apply what they learn than people who do not have this expectation. You need to be the champion of self-managing lifelong learning, not the enforcer of mandated, pushed learning. You need to model an approach to learning that is characterized by a growth mindset and helps people learn successfully.

The easiest way to make this happen is ensure that learners are anticipating what they will learn, why they will learn it, and what they will do with that information. They should have high but reasonable expectations for how they will apply what they learn to achieve business results. People that have a clear sense of the benefits and look forward to the experience are more likely to increase their knowledge, skills, and abilities, and take full advantage from the outset of their new knowledge and skills.

Be clear about what you expect them to learn, how you want them to apply that knowledge, and how that will make a difference for the organization. Let them know that you have high expectations, that you anticipate that they will improve performance in a significant way, and that you believe this will help the organization achieve its strategic goals.

Ask everyone in your organization to do the same. The message all employees need to see and hear is that learning is important, that everyone is expected to add to their knowledge, improve their skills, and grow as a person. Everyone includes managers at all levels. The new goal for an organization focused on managing minds is to remove any barriers to learning, such as maintaining bureaucratic silos of knowledge, hoarding information, discouraging employees from taking risks, and continuing to manage hands using the traditional command-and-control hierarchy. Anticipation in this new world demands an understanding that sharing knowledge is power, and whatever you learn can be successfully shared to the benefit of the whole organization.

Alliance

Learning in an organization requires what we call an alliance. That means that the people doing the learning, when it directly relates to the business, require support for what they have learned. That support can come from peers, team members, or managers. An employee's manager is an essential partner in the learning process. You need to learn how to be effective in your role of supporting continuous learning.

We have observed in our work that managers who are successful in helping people translate what they learn into measurable performance results are the same managers who have a strong learning relationship with their supervisors. These managers meet with their supervisors to discuss goals and the results of what they have learned. These are the managers who feel supported and believe that their participation in learning is important to the organization. They know that whatever they do to improve performance will be recognized and rewarded.

When there is a clear relationship between what is learned and the value and impact it can have on the business, the support of the manager is clear. Many of the companies we researched provide this support in a variety of ways—company-wide book review meetings, weekly learning reports, even presentations on what people have learned from a recent failure. At the very least, you need to have regular and frequent learning-focused conversations with the people on your team. Meet before they are about to learn something new, discuss what you expect from them, meet during the learning process to see how they are progressing, and at the end work with them to review what they learned and discuss how it can be used to achieve specific performance goals or meet a need in the organization.

For example, ask these questions when an employee chooses to take a course in a new programming language:

- What do you need to learn to help this organization achieve its business goals?
- How do you plan to learn what you need to know and do?
- How can I help you take the course, and is there anything else we can do to have what you learn in the course apply back at work, such as building a community of practice and connecting with others who have taken the course?
- What are your learning goals, and how will you and I know when they have been met?
- How will you determine that what you learned has been of value to the organization?
- What else can I do to support your learning and performance progress after the course?

The key to making this a successful relationship is to keep the focus on how you can help the employee learn and translate what the employee has learned into improved performance. In concert with the ideas related to managing minds, a learning alliance is all about communicating and collaborating with learners about what they are learning.

Application

For people to retain newly learned knowledge and skills, they must apply them soon after learning, before they start to fall too far off the learning curve. Whether building a team or solving a process problem, application of new knowledge and skills should occur within hours and days of learning, not within weeks and months, or never, as too often happens. This means that people must have meaningful opportunities to apply new learning. Managers and learners must plan together to ensure that learners have these opportunities—this cannot be left to chance.

For example, if employees are learning how to manage projects more effectively, make sure they have a project to manage and the ability to measure the outcomes of their performance. The project management skills will be lost if the employee waits days, weeks, or months to apply that new knowledge to a project. As you saw in the explanation of the learning curve and pivot point, forgetting sets in if learning is not reinforced through practice. This is as true with pull learning as it is with push training.

Accountability

When the intent of learning is to achieve business goals (as opposed to self-enrichment), employees are more likely to be successful if they are held accountable. This isn't about punishing failure; it's about learning from the experience.

Accountability means answering important evaluation questions. For example, what happened as a result of the learning process? Did it contribute to important business results? Was it worth the time, effort, and cost? Would the business goals have been achieved anyway? What needs to happen so that what was learned can contribute to important business results? Questions like these help people reflect on the learning process. The answers tell them what is working and what could be done differently to achieve success. Accountability for the learning process is as important as being accountable for results. Help employees be accountable for both.

Not all learning is directly linked to immediately measurable business or performance results. When the results are clearly tied to the business, it is not enough to believe that just showing up, passing tests, finishing the reading, or doing anything else at the start of the learning process will be effective. Compliance training programs, for example, suffer from the idea that attendance in a program means people are in compliance. The organization needs to manage and support all learning, and especially learning to meet specific business goals. Using the five *As* can help managers successfully manage the learning process and raise the odds that whatever is learned will be useful for the employee, the team, and the entire organization.

Assessing the Right Behaviors

To what extent is your organization a company that is managing minds? Before you can take your first step on your journey, you need to know where you're starting. Look around your organization. What do you see in different areas? What do you hear and read from different people? Do you think the company models managing minds behavior? Does the company practice a "do what I do" or a "do what I say" policy? How would you define your current culture?

These questions are not easy to answer, particularly if you work in a company that exclusively manages hands. In this case, assessing your culture is especially difficult because it is often unwritten and unspoken, the result of habits repeated over time. These managing hands cultures are defined by a "Because this is the way we always do it. Period." mentality. But just because these questions are difficult to answer does not make them any less important. Culture drives performance, and performance drives the company. If the culture implicitly or explicitly works against many of the conditions needed to manage minds, there's little chance of making a successful transition. If you want to become a culture that supports managing minds, you need to understand what the culture looks like today.

We have reviewed several tools that you can use to help understand how ready your culture is to support the principles and practices of managing minds. They look at the questions and answers from different directions and taken together can add up to a good snapshot of your current culture, your values about learning, and your readiness to be a company that is managing minds. Each of these surveys and questions can be led by a manager; however, it is best if they are presented by someone who has no stake in the outcome other than discovering the breadth and depth of the cultural attitudes and habits about learning.

Edgar Henry Schein, a former MIT Sloan School of Management professor, is best known for his work defining and changing organizational culture. Simply stated, Schein's definition and understanding of organizational culture is "a pattern of shared basic assumptions that was learned by a group as it solved its problems of external adaptation and internal integration, that has worked well enough to be considered valid and, therefore, to be taught to new members as the correct way to perceive, think, and feel in relation to those problems."[6] You will need to know to what extent the following exists to make your culture a managing hands or managing minds organization:

- How well do underlying beliefs and assumptions support managing minds?
- Do the values and principles drive a managing minds approach everywhere in your organization?
- Can everyone internally and externally see the symbols and artifacts of your organization as a company committed to managing minds?
- What are those symbols and artifacts?
- Does everyone know what they need to do to be successful?
- Do they know how to develop these competencies?
- Do they know how to sustain them over time?

An additional way to understand the kind of culture you have—managing hands, managing minds, or in transition—is a survey from David Garvin, Amy Edmondson, and Francesca Gino, professors at Harvard Business School. They say the tool should be strictly used for learning about the culture, not to judge the quality of an organization. Their specific survey questions result in feedback for organizational reflection. By collecting the data and then discussing the findings, you can deal with the critical question of what kind of culture you have. When applying their survey to managing minds, we would ask the organization:

- Does your culture support managing minds?
- Do you have everyday processes and procedures in place to ensure that managing minds, push learning, communication, and collaboration are embedded in the way everyone works together?

- Do your top leaders make continuous learning a priority and communicate this throughout the organization?[7]

Leaders at all levels of the organization, after discovering the answers to these three questions, can motivate learning, improve performance, and contribute to developing a culture that supports managing minds in the process.

One of our colleagues, Jim Stilwell, provides some informative and useful ideas for using conversations initiated by these tools and surveys to begin promoting change in your company. He looks at four important steps that can turn the questions and answers into actions:[8]

1. Senior leadership must communicate a compelling need for the survey in advance of sending out the questionnaires. As a part of this communication, senior leaders should clearly define the entire data gathering and feedback process, emphasizing the fact that the people answering the questions need to take time to reflect and review their answers.

2. The findings from the survey will benefit from clarification and validation by the people who provided the survey responses. They need to review the answers and make sure they represent their views.

3. Discussing the findings with groups at all levels of the company for their interpretation and recommendations leads to a deeper understanding of the answers, greater alignment throughout the company, and better solutions for everyone.

4. Leaders must communicate back to the entire organization what will be done as a result of the insights gained through the surveys and group discussions. This communication should clearly define what leaders know now that they did not know before the survey. They need to point out what will be changed, how it will make the company more successful, and why. Leaders need to assign people to be responsible for the changes and let them know the timetable for when those changes will take place. Finally, and perhaps most important, leaders must describe exactly how the follow-up will happen to ensure that the changes have been successful.

Organizational assessments can help you in your journey to becoming a company that manages minds. They can tell you where you are at a point in time—the latitude and longitude of your cultural ideas, customs, values, and social behavior as it relates to learning. Once you have that position pinpointed, you will be able to select the best route to becoming a managing minds company. You can see the direction you need to go to begin supporting and encouraging the continuous and collective discovery, sharing, adopting, and applying knowledge and skills at the individual, team, and organizational levels. Appendices 1 and 2 offer two organizational assessments to determine your and your organization's readiness to manage minds.

8

WORKPLACES OF TOMORROW

We think that the heart of managing minds was summed up years ago by Antoine de Saint-Exupéry, who was a keen observer of the relationship of hands and minds at work. He is thought to have said, "If you want to build a ship, don't drum up people to collect wood and don't assign them tasks and work, but rather teach them to long for the endless immensity of the sea."

We cannot anticipate the turbulent seas and uncharted territory ahead in the economy, but we can prepare managers for navigating their organizations to success.

Imagine that we have traveled to the not-too-distant future. All organizations are managing minds, from the most high-tech companies to the oldest factories and mills. What would a day be like? Imagine a company in which:

- Continuous learning, and learning fast, is key, even in the face of unprecedented change: managing tremendous amounts of information, creating new products and processes in response to global competition, using new apps to be more efficient and effective, and responding to the learning preferences of a multigenerational, diverse workforce.

- Employees are hired because they are excited about learning and improving themselves. They have a history of taking responsibility for their own learning. They aren't afraid to admit that they do not know something, and they willingly seek out the help they need to improve and become high performers.

- The message from the CEO to new employees is that learning and self-development are highly valued. Continuous learning is expected from everyone in the organization, from senior leadership down. Incentives and public recognition reward those employees who seek out opportunities to enhance their competencies and increase their capability to contribute to the success of the organization.

- Critical information is easily accessible on the go. Equipment operators can view safety information on their smartphones when and where they need it. Managers can download coaching advice prior to meeting with a direct report. Leaders can see a video on open-book management just before discussing it with their teams.

- Managers meet every few weeks with their direct reports to discuss performance and learning goals. Employees report what they've been learning. Managers give employees constructive feedback, and together they decide how to achieve goals. Managers provide opportunities for employees to practice newly acquired skills and put into practice what they've been learning.

- Team leaders ask for feedback on their leadership. They discuss their communication, delegation, coaching, team facilitation, and planning with team members. Team leaders are constantly improving the effectiveness of team meetings and modeling meeting management for team members. Together, they are learning how to facilitate and contribute to meetings that are engaging and productive.

- Leaders of projects conduct an after-action review at the completion of each project. Project team members discuss what happened, how it happened, the results, how that compares with what the project was intended to accomplish, successes and failures, and what should be done differently in the future. Project managers and team members put these lessons learned into practice on their next projects.
- Organization-wide strategic planning is seen as an opportunity for learning. Participants are asked to discuss the strengths and weaknesses of the planning process. Leaders and managers use that feedback to improve the organization's strategic planning process, and this new process is standardized in the organization.
- People start their workday with an attitude that can be described as fearless, looking forward to using their minds to contribute to the success and happiness of their organization.

There is a purpose to imagining a company in which people are managing minds. The current neuroscience theory is that we use the past as a scaffold to build an image of the future; the way we did things in the past helps determine what we will do in the future. But the biggest problem any organization has when it tries to change is the inability to imagine a different way of doing things. So imagining a company in which we are managing minds, doing things very differently from when we were managing hands, is necessary if we are to get from here to there, from today to a better future.

The Timeframe for Change

There is a cost for everything. If you're open to the idea that the cost of moving toward managing minds is worth the investment—time, money, and effort—then the blueprint is here in these pages. Although there is a cost to change, the cost of not changing is far greater.

Even a small company can begin to adopt ideas in this book. Inform everyone in the company that, as a manager, you want to manage minds, not hands, and there will be changes. Outline the changes you are considering. List some of the ideas you found in this book. Listen to the reactions people have, find out what new ideas they bring to the table, unleash the power of their minds, and see where it goes. See how many more pieces of the puzzle you can put into play.

If you are a large corporation and just getting started, choose a small department or even a group in a department. Tell them what you are planning to do and what it will mean. Let them react. Listen. Ask for ideas. Present a list of ideas. Let them react. Listen. Ask for ways that they can improve the product you make, and see how many people have courses and programs they want to take not only for their professional growth, but for their personal interests. Find out what they think.

More important, discover what they imagine. How can we do a better job working with our customers? What can we do to make our products better? Who has an idea for ways to make our customer service awesome? Now that everyone knows and is responsible for the bottom line, what are the first three things we can do to increase profits, improve performance, or reduce costs? (Pick one to start.) And then add, how can we do a better job at training and learning? What is working and what needs to be changed? What needs to happen to help us manage minds?

The Risk and the Reward

There is a lot to consider when thinking about the risk and the reward of moving toward a managing minds model for your company. Edgar Schein spelled out the problem when he said, "The rate of technological, economic, political, and sociocultural change is increasing, and organizations are, therefore, finding it more and more important to figure out how to adapt."[1]

Adaptation in turbulent environments involves more than minor adjustments. It often requires genuinely innovative thrusts: new missions, new goals, new products and services, new ways of getting things done, and even new values and assumptions. Most important, adaptation involves managing perpetual change. Organizations will need to figure out how to learn continuously and be open to constantly changing.

The difficulty is that organizations are by nature, and often by design, oriented toward stabilizing and routinizing work. The risks are that any movement in your company toward managing minds will fail. That's good. In a managing minds company, every failure is a lesson. The initial risk can be mitigated by starting small and building on each success. The rewards have been demonstrated in each of the business case examples presented in this book. Almost every company we studied that has decided to switch from managing hands to managing minds, or that started out as a managing minds company, has done so successfully. Startups may have an advantage because they are younger and do not need to change habitual ways of managing and learning, but established companies have more reasons to change if they want to survive.

Marcia L. Conner and James G. Clawson, in their book, *Creating a Learning Culture*, write this about the risk of not moving toward a company that is focused on learning:

> Today it seems that organizations need to be able to do
> more than just adapt: they must become agile in the face of
> constantly changing conditions. And if organizations are to
> respond intelligently, they must make learning a central part of
> their strategy for survival and growth. If they do not, the future
> looks more and more bleak; it will just be a matter of time. If,
> however, leaders and the people within the organization are
> learning all the time, faster than competitors, and applying the
> right strategies at the right times, the organization has hope.[2]

We think the best statement about the issue of the risk and reward is summed up in this imagined conversation between two executives thinking about the cost of the investment and the change:

> **CFO to CEO:** "What happens if we invest all this money into managing minds and they leave us?"
>
> **CEO to CFO:** "What happens if we don't and they stay?"

Break From the Past

Change is always hard, but not for the reasons most of us believe. Neuroscience has proven that we use the same part of our brain to remember the past and create the future. We use the past to fill in the scaffolding for the future, to maintain continuity between those two imagined points in time. Evolution has made sure that our brains work this way because in the past our survival depended on the future being predictable, stable, and understandable. We are not designed for change.

Unfortunately, we are no longer simple hunter-gatherers. We live in a world so different that even the speed of change itself has changed. Until the 16th century, it took 1,500 years for human knowledge to double. Now, that number has been reduced to one to two years, and it is shrinking to six to 12 months.[3] The map that this book has drawn between the old and the new is clear: Companies must change. Companies must stop managing hands and begin to manage minds. Company leadership must let go of a past that no longer works to imagine a future in which they can succeed.

There are always visionaries among us. They are untethered from the past and thus free to imagine the future. Their only question is not "How?" or "When?" but "Why?" Why are we doing the same thing tomorrow the same way we did it yesterday?

In the mid-1980s, Ricardo Stemler returned to his home city of Sao Paolo with his new MBA degree from Harvard. He took over Semco, the company his father had built, which manufactured centrifuges for use in the vegetable oils industry. Just 10 years later, Semler had achieved 500 percent growth in profits, 600 percent growth in revenues, and a 700 percent increase in productivity. At the same time, employee turnover plummeted to 2 percent, versus the industry average of nearly 20 percent. By the early 2000s, Semco's sales were in excess of $400 million, and the company had interests in other businesses worth approximately $9 billion.

Semler achieved all this by questioning and consciously dismantling everything he learned at Harvard about managing a business. He moved away from managing hands and started managing minds. He realized that the key to growth is the ability to break away from the way business has been done in the past and reimagine new and better ways that business can be done in the future. He began directly challenging all the assumptions that corporations throughout the world held sacred at the time. The conclusions he came to, and the changes he implemented some 30 years ago, still seem amazingly revolutionary.

Semler wondered why his company was spending precious resources babysitting employees like infants or tracking them like criminals. After all, his employees and their ability to think, solve problems, and ask questions were his company's greatest asset, and his company had freely chosen to hire them. If employment is a contract by which an employer agrees to compensate an employee for a certain amount of work, then why should it matter what time an employee begins or ends that work or how many days they take off? Are you paying for their hands or their minds? As long as the work is done on time, what difference does it make?

And, what does a company gain by demanding that employees spend hours each day commuting to and from the corporate offices if they can work efficiently somewhere else? To make better use of this time and help employees grow, he instituted the Rush Hour MBA program, which uses the two hours many people would spend commuting to lead a study session on running the business. Managing minds often means finding creative ways to help people learn.

All employees at Semco shared in the company profits, so why not let them decide their own compensation? Semler made it easy for employees to access and understand financial information on what colleagues at Semco and competitor companies were earning, the cost of benefits, and corporate margins so they could make smart and informed decisions. He was practicing open-book management before the term was coined.

If employees no longer get satisfaction from their job, why not find them a new one within the company rather than lose a good employee? If they want to travel or pursue another interest or look after a sick relative, why not give them the option to "buy back" some of their time? Happy and engaged employees who are completely focused on their work do better work than those who are unhappy or distracted.

Finally, employees were actively encouraged to do what Semler did in the very beginning: repeatedly ask why. There is no reason set in stone to do anything. Why should everyone be in the same place at the same time, why do we need titles to do our jobs, why should only a few people know how the company is doing? The "why" question even comes up in meetings, when people think, "Why are we having this meeting?" As Semler says in his TED Talk, "When people are not only free, but actively encouraged, to question, to get up and leave a meeting that bores them, to pop into a meeting that interests them, and to push back on previous conclusions, you actually have a chance to get to the heart of the matter, to escape ruts, and to do something that's worth doing."[4]

These managing minds characteristics can be found in many of the businesses we profiled in this book, but Semco stands out for two reasons. First, it is the poster company for managing minds because it has successfully used the managing minds approach with every employee at every level of the company and has been far more successful than any of its competitors. Second, it started this journey in the mid-1980s.

By having the courage to untether Semco from the habitual management models of the past, Semler was free to imagine a new and better future. As he puts it, "Just stop everything and try doing something else, trusting that it will be okay—and much better than what you're doing simply because you're stuck in an existing process."[5]

The Key to Change

Oberg Industries of Freeport, Pennsylvania, manufactures precision components and tooling from a variety of materials used by Fortune 500 companies and other leading manufacturers throughout the world. As the company began to automate and sell into a global market, Donald E. Oberg, the company's founder, realized that simply managing hands would no longer be effective as the company evolved.

Oberg saw the value of managing minds and began an apprenticeship program that has become a model for other manufacturing companies worldwide. The values of the program, which has trained more than 1,000 employees, are straightforward and simple:

- Establish a culture of continuous learning for employees who need to maintain their skills and knowledge to effectively act as mentors in the apprenticeship program.

- Introduce new employees to the managing minds culture so they understand the value and importance of continuous learning, communication, and collaboration.
- Put the Oberg brand at the top of the industry and recognize the excellence of Oberg employees, who are up-to-date high performers.

Has the move toward managing minds been worth the investment? According to the company, graduates are recognized as among the very best at what they do; they have also become company executives, sales managers, engineers, quality managers, estimators, project managers, or production supervisors. Some have even started their own companies.[6]

"We will always maintain our apprenticeship program because we value our highly engaged, creative, and innovative people," Oberg says. "We've seen a triple-digit return on investment from our apprentice graduates even during difficult economic conditions."[7]

Oberg's story illustrates the key to this or any major organizational change: It starts at the top. If the person running the group, department, or company does not fully believe that this is the right way to run the organization, then it will not work. In every company, leaders lead by example. In companies taking small steps toward managing minds to those that are fully committed leaders, they believed that the direction was correct and necessary to compete and perform at the highest level possible.

Managing minds is becoming the new normal, even though its parts have received more attention than the whole. The discussion has ranged from the training needs of Millennials to the importance of foosball tables and gourmet food in the cafeterias. It has included seminars, webinars, and workshops that focused on every topic, from delivering training in smaller chunks to making presentations more interactive to the need for collaborative workspaces. We see these pieces discussed and written about every day. They indicate a desire to make the workplace more engaging and productive. What managers are realizing is that it's not about events and perks; it's about making a profound cultural shift from managing hands to managing minds.

THE PAIN AND HOPE OF THE GREAT DISLOCATION

We didn't set out to change the way we manage people and the ways they learn. We just discovered that these changes were already occurring all over the world, but not many seemed to have noticed.

In 1972, using a tape recorder and his insatiable curiosity, Studs Terkel traveled around America and talked with working people about their jobs. The result was a landmark book titled *Working: People Talk About What They Do All Day and How They Feel About What They Do.*[1]

In 2016, the raw, unedited tapes were broadcast on NPR in a series they called "Working Then and Now."[2] The interview that stands out for us is a conversation with Gary Bryner. In the original interview in 1972, Gary talked with Studs about being a union member in the 1970s and what it meant to work in an automobile factory.

At that time, we were in the early part of the transition from people building cars to robots assembling them faster, more effectively, and more efficiently. This meant that fewer and fewer people were needed to make cars, and the people who were left in the factories needed to be smarter about their jobs. The Terkel interview is a snapshot of people going through one of the great dislocations that occur every time there is a structural shift in the workplace resulting from a change in an economic paradigm. Here's the interview:

STUDS TERKEL: I am somewhere between Youngstown and Warren, Ohio. This is [an] industrial area—steel, automobiles—talking to Gary Bryner. Gary Bryner is the president of Local 1114 United Auto Workers—no—1124.

GARY BRYNER: One-one-one-two.

TERKEL: One-one-one-two—well, what sort of plant is this?

BRYNER: It's the General Motors Vega plant in Lordstown.

TERKEL: The most automated plant in the world, isn't it?

BRYNER: Right. It's the fastest line speed in the world, and they've got the most modern equipment—the Unimates. They got 22 in a row, 11 on each side of the line.

TERKEL: Can you describe the Unimate?

BRYNER: Well, it looks like a robot, you know? And it reminds me of a praying mantis. When they took the Unimates on, we were building 60 an hour prior to the Unimates, and when we came back to work with the Unimates, we were building 101 cars per hour. See; they never tire. They never sweat. They never complain. They never miss work. They're always there.

TERKEL: Yeah, so what happened to the guys in the plant that are working there now?

BRYNER: It's a funny thing, you know? When they revamp the plant, they try to take every movement out of the guy's day so that he could conserve seconds and time so they can make him more efficient, more productive.

TERKEL: Is the assembly line approach dependent upon the fact that each guy is exactly like the other guy?

BRYNER: Right. GM's reason for trying to be more efficient is if they could take one second and save a second on each guy's effort, they would over a year make a million dollars.

TERKEL: One second.

BRYNER: That's right. You know, they use the stopwatches, and they say, look; we know from experience that it takes so many seconds to walk from here to there. We know that it takes so many seconds to shoot that screw. We know the gun turns so fast and screw's so long and the hole's so deep. We know how long it takes, and that's what that guy's going to do.

And our argument has always been, you know, that's mechanical. That's not human. Look; we tire. We sweat. We have hangovers. We have upset stomachs. We have feelings, emotions, and we're not about to be placed in a category of a machine.

In the industrial economy, a company's unstated goal was to turn people into machines, until they were no longer needed, because there were machines to replace them. As we were writing this book and thinking about the knowledge economy, we never forgot about the people who have been hurt by the structural and seemingly unstoppable shift between these two economic eras.

Historically, great shifts in the way we work, brought about by changes in economic paradigms, cause profound, tectonic structural changes that produce dislocations in the workforce. In each of the previous dislocations, people could move from one job to another. For example, workers delivering ice could study HVAC at night school and become refrigerator repairman; a radio repairman could become a television salesman. When one job disappeared, there was always another regardless of education level, work experience, or skills.

That has changed; there isn't necessarily any place to go. This great dislocation has caused millions of people to stop working. They might not be educated to the point where they are capable of learning the new technological and social skills needed in companies today; their old jobs have been taken over by something digital, or their hands have been replaced by machines. Once, their level of education, skills, experience, and hard-work ethic was more than good enough for a company in the industrial economy. Suddenly it no longer counts for anything. It's not just that they think that they are no longer useful; they really are no longer useful in the knowledge economy.

In 2016, Georgetown University's Center on Education and the Workforce published an extensive report revealing that "while the US created 11.6 million new jobs after the recession, 11.5 million of those went to individuals with at least some college education."[3] According to the report, the recent recession "decimated low-skill blue-collar and clerical jobs. Industries like manufacturing and construction have shrunk; office and administrative support positions—a primary source of work for non-college grads—have also dwindled, thanks to the rise of automation and digital information storage."[4] In the 2015 Forrester forecast, they noted that "by 2019, 25% of all job tasks will be offloaded to software robots, physical robots, or customer self-service automation."[5] The report also predicts that by 2025, 16 percent of the current jobs in America will simply disappear.[6] We consider this a conservative estimate due to the exponential rate of change.

These changes are happening at the structural level of the economy and are irreversible. These jobs are not coming back. The question is what to do to help the people who have been displaced. In the United States alone, we've heard a long and growing list of solutions that include redistributing wealth, designing retraining programs that provide skills needed for tomorrow's workforce, ending stock buybacks and offshoring manufacturing jobs, leveling the playing field so companies do not compete with countries that subsidize production, reducing the 40-hour workweek to 35 or 30 hours, phasing in new technologies in less disruptive ways, lowering the Medicare eligibility age to cover more displaced workers, providing a universal basic income for those workers who cannot find their way back into the workforce, granting free higher education to those same workers' children, offering a variety of incentives for technology and innovation centers to be in small towns in the heartland, and more. Some, all, or none of these may be the answer.

We acknowledge that this latest paradigm shift to a new economy is causing great pain, perhaps more so than with any previous dislocation. Too many good people lost their livelihood, their hopes, and their dreams as their jobs disappeared. We want to be certain that the people most negatively affected by the transition are seen and heard, understood and supported by those who have the power to bring companies into the new knowledge economy.

We do not underestimate how difficult this will be. Work in this new economy is a young person's game played at the edge of your ability to innovate and create, experiment and fail, manage your own learning, curate information, use the latest technology to find what you need to know and do, collaborate and communicate, reinvent yourself, and adopt and adapt your job description to the ever-changing needs of the business. Jeff Bezos of Amazon often gives a speech he calls "It's Still Day One." In that talk, he reminds employees "never to rest on their laurels, no matter how successful they were."[7] Amazon is a company that has been reinventing itself for more than 20 years, always working as if today is still day one. Amazon has learned that a company in the knowledge economy cannot stop and react to whatever surprises tomorrow has in store. The company and every employee must always be proactive, continuously learning, imagining, and reinventing themselves to make that future happen.

These new knowledge economy companies are being forced to learn how to manage the way people think, process information, and make decisions to survive and thrive in the new global, digital, hyper-competitive economy. We believe that people who can adapt to this new management environment will have successful and satisfying careers. Our hope is that these new companies will be kinder, gentler, and more concerned about how they affect their workers, their families, and the communities. These companies can choose to be more socially responsible and environmentally sustainable, with a stronger moral compass than their predecessors. They are dealing with the whole person; to them, the idea of work-life balance is no longer a seesaw, but a circle in which work is a part of a life.

New and better technologies and improved business practices appear all the time. You cannot keep doing what you have always done hoping it just keeps working as it always did. That is magical thinking. In the knowledge economy, trying to maintain the status quo becomes a company's obituary. You need to keep learning and changing.

We hope *Minds at Work* can be a map that shows you what this new workscape looks like, and how to shift to a new way of managing that is helping create some of the world's most successful companies.

MANAGING MINDS DNA ASSESSMENT

The Managing Minds DNA Assessment determines the extent to which you, the people with whom you work, and your entire organization are managing minds. The assessment is most effective when taken by different individuals, who can then compare their answers and experiences and arrive at a collective evaluation first for each question and then for the entire assessment.

As you read each statement, think about how often it is true, and award the associated number of points. Choose the response to each statement that is closest to what you have experienced. A perfect score is 100.

1. The message from leaders (CEO, senior executives, and others) in the organization is that continuous learning by individuals, teams, and the whole organization is highly valued.
   o Always True = 5 Points
   o Often True = 4 Points
   o Sometimes True = 3 Points
   o Rarely True = 2 Points
   o Never True = 1 Point

2. Leaders communicate their expectation that people will apply what they learn to achieving the goals of the organization.
   o Always True = 5 Points

- Often True = 4 Points
- Sometimes True = 3 Points
- Rarely True = 2 Points
- Never True = 1 Point

3. Leaders across the organization have a growth mindset. They believe that any employee can learn, grow, and change within the organization given the right experiences and feedback.
   - Always True = 5 Points
   - Often True = 4 Points
   - Sometimes True = 3 Points
   - Rarely True = 2 Points
   - Never True = 1 Point

4. All employees are given opportunities for continuous development of knowledge and skills.
   - Always True = 5 Points
   - Often True = 4 Points
   - Sometimes True = 3 Points
   - Rarely True = 2 Points
   - Never True = 1 Point

5. Information is stored in a place that is easily accessible by everyone in the organization, such as a database.
   - Always True = 5 Points
   - Often True = 4 Points
   - Sometimes True = 3 Points
   - Rarely True = 2 Points
   - Never True = 1 Point

6. People in the organization use information from the database to acquire new knowledge and know-how.
   - Always True = 5 Points
   - Often True = 4 Points
   - Sometimes True = 3 Points
   - Rarely True = 2 Points
   - Never True = 1 Point

7. People take risks and experiment with new ideas and methods for the purpose of learning.

- o Always True = 5 Points
- o Often True = 4 Points
- o Sometimes True = 3 Points
- o Rarely True = 2 Points
- o Never True = 1 Point

8. Managers foster risk-taking behavior by recognizing the effort and learning even if the results are unsatisfactory.
   - o Always True = 5 Points
   - o Often True = 4 Points
   - o Sometimes True = 3 Points
   - o Rarely True = 2 Points
   - o Never True = 1 Point

9. Application of learning in the workplace is measured and evaluated.
   - o Always True = 5 Points
   - o Often True = 4 Points
   - o Sometimes True = 3 Points
   - o Rarely True = 2 Points
   - o Never True = 1 Point

10. Managers recognize people for acquiring and using new knowledge and skills.
    - o Always True = 5 Points
    - o Often True = 4 Points
    - o Sometimes True = 3 Points
    - o Rarely True = 2 Points
    - o Never True = 1 Point

11. Everyone is encouraged to be reflective about what they are learning and doing, individually and in teams.
    - o Always True = 5 Points
    - o Often True = 4 Points
    - o Sometimes True = 3 Points
    - o Rarely True = 2 Points
    - o Never True = 1 Point

12. Managers are continually asking people how they can improve what they are doing.

- Always True = 5 Points
- Often True = 4 Points
- Sometimes True = 3 Points
- Rarely True = 2 Points
- Never True = 1 Point

13. Managers communicate how acquiring specific knowledge and skills will contribute to the success of the organization.
    - Always True = 5 Points
    - Often True = 4 Points
    - Sometimes True = 3 Points
    - Rarely True = 2 Points
    - Never True = 1 Point

14. People understand how what they learn is aligned with important results for the organization.
    - Always True = 5 Points
    - Often True = 4 Points
    - Sometimes True = 3 Points
    - Rarely True = 2 Points
    - Never True = 1 Point

15. People in work units are encouraged by managers to share what they learned with other units.
    - Always True = 5 Points
    - Often True = 4 Points
    - Sometimes True = 3 Points
    - Rarely True = 2 Points
    - Never True = 1 Point

16. Information flows freely throughout organization, regardless of the department where it was generated.
    - Always True = 5 Points
    - Often True = 4 Points
    - Sometimes True = 3 Points
    - Rarely True = 2 Points
    - Never True = 1 Point

17. Managers accept responsibility for employee learning and performance improvement.
    o Always True = 5 Points
    o Often True = 4 Points
    o Sometimes True = 3 Points
    o Rarely True = 2 Points
    o Never True = 1 Point

18. Managers encourage people they manage to acquire new knowledge and skills and develop competencies that make them more valuable to the organization.
    o Always True = 5 Points
    o Often True = 4 Points
    o Sometimes True = 3 Points
    o Rarely True = 2 Points
    o Never True = 1 Point

19. The organization recruits and hires people who show a capacity and motivation to continue learning.
    o Always True = 5 Points
    o Often True = 4 Points
    o Sometimes True = 3 Points
    o Rarely True = 2 Points
    o Never True = 1 Point

20. Managers promote people who continually acquire new knowledge and skills, learn from their successes and failures, take risks for the purpose of learning, and are always trying to develop themselves.
    o Always True = 5 Points
    o Often True = 4 Points
    o Sometimes True = 3 Points
    o Rarely True = 2 Points
    o Never True = 1 Point

Add up your points and compare the total to the descriptions below.

- **100-81 points:** Congratulations! Leaders are managing minds across the company. The success and benefits will only get better. Your company is in what we define as the aspirational zone.

- **80-61 points:** Your company is moving in the right direction. Managing minds is becoming an integral part of the day-to-day business. Make sure the leadership does more to actively promote the idea and watch your score climb. You are high transitional.

- **60-41 points:** Some people in your company are managing minds. The leadership level needs to get onboard and communicate and build on any successes to see the score jump and realize more of the benefits. You are functioning as starting transitional.

- **40 points or less:** Your company is taking a scattershot approach to managing minds, and needs to focus on the idea as individuals and teams find ways to do more until the score starts to improve. Your organization is still in the 20th century and is acting as if you can continue to do business as you always have.

APPENDIX 2

ORGANIZATION LEARNING MATURITY SCALE

The organizational learning maturity scale can be taken with a cross-functional group of employees from different levels and departments to discuss the following questions and answers. The group's answers are not as important as the conversations generated by the questions about what it means to be a company managing minds. While the focus is exclusively on learning, which is at the heart of a managing minds organization, the answers will highlight the basic conditions needed in a culture to even attempt managing minds.

The assessment is composed of 20 statements grouped into four categories. The group needs to choose and agree on the statement that best describes the current practices in the company for each category.

1. In terms of individual learning:	Score
Training and development programs are topical, off the shelf, and event-based.	1
Learning activities are designed to develop the knowledge, skills, attitudes, and beliefs needed by individuals to achieve results in the workplace; training is customized and delivered when needed.	2
Learning activities are aligned with the organization's strategic goals; people can see how acquiring new knowledge and skills will make them more effective in the organization.	3

Individuals have developed learning plans with their managers; learning activities encourage feedback and reflection; individual beliefs and values are addressed; managers are supportive.	4
Expectations for ongoing learning are made clear to new hires and other stakeholders; knowledge and skills are shared freely among employees and other stakeholders; people experiment and take risks; individual learning is recognized and rewarded; a wide variety of learning methods are utilized.	5

2. In terms of team learning:	Score
Team training, if it happens at all, is generic; team goals do not include learning; teams do not work on improving team functioning.	1
Teams evaluate themselves based on intended outcomes achieved; teams seek to learn why they did or did not achieve intended outcomes; teams try to improve performance.	2
Teams understand the vision and mission of the organization; teams are continually evaluating themselves based on achieving organizational goals; teams learn from experience.	3
Teams have learning plans; teams receive tailored training in teamwork; teams regularly assess their own effectiveness as a team and try to improve teamwork and work processes.	4
Teams apply action learning; teams continually assess performance and use this information to improve; teams share knowledge with other teams; teams make learning one of their goals; teams regularly collect and use feedback from customers and other stakeholders.	5

3. In terms of whole organization learning:	Score
There are no whole organization learning activities.	1
The organization evaluates its performance, but this is not reported to people.	2
Groups of internal and external stakeholders review the organization's performance in relation to strategic goals; improvements are made.	3
Employees and other stakeholders share a vision for the direction of the organization; systems are in place for sharing knowledge; collecting and learning from feedback is recognized and rewarded.	4
Learning is an explicit goal of the organization; a knowledge management system facilitates sharing of information among individuals and teams; knowledge is readily shared across departments; physical space is conducive to learning among individuals and within teams; underlying values related to actions are continually examined.	5

4. In terms of community learning:	Score
There are no community learning activities.	1
Employees conduct a community needs assessment; employees talk to community members about topics of mutual interest.	2
Employees learn how to work with community members to set goals and develop a strategy to achieve those goals.	3
Employees and community members establish a system for continually assessing needs, establishing goals, and analyzing outcomes; there is regular community feedback and reflection.	4
The organization has a dynamic learning relationship with the community; the organization and community are continually learning about the assets of the community and how they can be used to improve quality of life; knowledge is freely shared among the organization and the community stakeholders; the organization helps the community learn how to learn about itself.	5

After you have selected a statement from each of the four groupings, add up the value of these four statements. Your total score will fall between four and 20 points:

- **Four to eight points** indicates an organization that does not yet value learning and is not yet ready to begin functioning like a company that is managing minds.
- **Nine to 16 points** indicates an organization that cares about learning but has not yet made learning a daily and constant part of its culture.
- **Seventeen to 20 points** indicates a company that fully supports learning and is well on its way to managing minds.

These point totals are rough indicators of the readiness of your culture to begin managing minds. The greatest value of this exercise is starting the conversations about learning and managing minds in your organization.

NOTES

Introduction

1. Korn Ferry, "Korn Ferry Global Study: Majority of CEOs See More Value in Technology Than Their Workforce," Korn Ferry (November 17, 2016): www.kornferry.com/press/korn-ferry -global-study-majority of ceos see-more-value-in-technology-than -their-workforce.

2. John Noble Wilford, *The Mapmakers: The Story of the Great Pioneers in Cartography—From Antiquity to the Space Age* (New York: Knopf, 1981).

3. Beth Waterhouse, "A Sustainable Future?" Public Broadcasting Company (n.d.): www.pbs.org/ktca/farmhouses/sustainable _future.html.

4. Ibid.

5. Justin Ferriman, "The History of Training and Development," LearnDash (April 6, 2016): www.learndash.com/history-of -training-and-development.

6. Ibid.

7. The Takeaway, "Robert Reich: Trump's Jobs Plan Misguided in Era of Globalization," The Takeaway (February 28, 2017): www.wnyc .org/story/can-president-trump-create-jobs-he-promised-bring- back.

8. Michael Chui, James Manyika, and Mehdi Miremadi, "Four Fundamentals of Workplace Automation," *McKinsey Quarterly* (November 2015): www.mckinsey.com/business-functions /digital-mckinsey/our-insights/four-fundamentals-of-workplace -automation.

9. Organisation for Economic Co-Operation and Development (OECD), *The Knowledge Based Economy* (Paris: OECD, 1996): www.oecd.org/sti/sci-tech/1913021.pdf.
10. Quentin Hardy, "Gearing Up for the Cloud, AT&T Tells Its Workers: Adapt, or Else," *New York Times* (February 13, 2016): www.nytimes.com/2016/02/14/technology/gearing-up-for-the -cloud-att-tells-its-workers-adapt-or-else.html.
11. Ibid.
12. Ibid.

Chapter 1

1. Kim Gittleson, "Can a Company Live Forever?" BBC News (January 18, 2012): www.bbc.com/news/business-16611040.
2. Scott D. Anthony, S. Patrick Viguerie, and Andrew Waldeck, "Corporate Longevity: Turbulence Ahead for Large Organizations," Innosight Executive Briefing (Spring 2016): www .innosight.com/wp-content/uploads/2016/08/Corporate -Longevity-2016-Final.pdf.
3. Michael Beer and Russell A. Eisenstat, "The Silent Killers of Strategy Implementation and Learning," MIT Sloan Management Review (July 15, 2000): http://sloanreview.mit.edu/article /the-silent-killers-of-strategy-implementation-and-learning.
4. Peter A.C. Smith and Tom Cockburn, *Impact of Emerging Digital Technologies on Leadership in Global Business* (Hershey, PA: Business Science Reference, 2014).
5. Maur Judkis, "A Robot Named Bruno Helped Make Your Pizza. Is It Still 'Artisanal'?" *Washington Post* (November 1, 2016): www .washingtonpost.com/lifestyle/food/artisanal-pizza-made -by-bruno-the-robot-and-other-true-tales-of-automated -food/2016/10/31/2ba482dc-9a0d-11e6-b3c9-f662adaa0048 _story.html?utm_term=.97471f528327.
6. Jane Wakefield, "Foxconn Replaces '60,000 Factory Workers With Robots,'" BBC News (May 25, 2016): www.bbc.com/news /technology-36376966.

7. Rafi Letzter, "Wendy's Is Replacing Its Lowest-Paid Workers With Robots," *Business Insider* (May 13, 2016): www.techinsider.io/wendys-workers-will-lose-jobs-to-robots-2016-5.

8. Fred Lambert, "Tesla Gigafactory: A Look at the Robots and 'Machine Building the Machine' at the Battery Factory," *Electrek* (July 31, 2016): https://electrek.co/2016/07/31/tesla-gigafactory-robots-machines-battery-factory.

9. Jeff Kavanaugh, "Why Your Leadership Skills Won't Get You Hired (But These Four Other Things Might)," *Fast Company* (March 6, 2017): www.fastcompany.com/3068705/why-your-leadership-skills-wont-get-you-hired-but-these-four-other-things-m.

10. Anthony Abbatiello, Marjorie Knight, Stacey Philpot, and Indranil Roy, "Leadership Disrupted: Pushing the Boundaries," Deloitte University Press (February 28, 2017): https://dupress.deloitte.com/dup-us-en/focus/human-capital-trends/2017/developing-digital-leaders.html.

11. Stanford University, Redesigning Work for 21st Century Men and Women (class, Stanford University, Stanford, CA, 2014-2015).

12. Arie de Geus, "Planning as Learning," *Harvard Business Review* (March 1988): https://hbr.org/1988/03/planning-as-learning.

13. Association for Talent Development (ATD), *State of the Industry* (Alexandria, VA: ATD Press, 2016).

14. Stephen J. Gill, "Still Too Much Reliance on Instructor-Led, Event-Based Employee Training," The Performance Improvement Blog (March 17, 2014): http://stephenjgill.typepad.com/performance_improvement_b/2014/03/still-too-much-reliance-on-instructor-led-event-based-employee-training.html.

15. American Society for Training & Development (ASTD), *State of the Industry* (Alexandria, VA: ASTD Press: 2013).

16. In 2013, 70 percent of training was instructor-led; we reached $92 billion by multiplying that percentage by the $164.2 billion spent on training in 2013, which was then multiplied by the 80 percent of participants not applying learning from this training to the job. ([0.70 × $164.2 billion] × 0.80 = $92 billion).

17. Clark Quinn, "The Great eLearning Garbage Vortex," Learnlets (December 15, 2009): http://blog.learnlets.com/2009/12 /the-great-elearning-garbage-vortex.

Chapter 2

1. Mats Alvesson and André Spicer, *The Stupidity Paradox: The Power and Pitfalls of Functional Stupidity at Work* (London: Profile Books, 2017).
2. Yuki Noguchi, "Businesses Try to Stave Off Brain Drain as Boomers Retire," NPR (January 15, 2015): www.npr .org/2015/01/15/377201540/businesses-try-to-stave-off-brain -drain-as-boomers-retire.
3. Gallup, "Gallup Daily: U.S. Employee Engagement," Gallup (accessed April 3, 2017): www.gallup.com/poll/180404/gallup -daily-employee-engagement.aspx.
4. Joost Minnaar and Pim de Morree, "These 3 Practical Changes Boosted the Success and Happiness at UKTV," Corporate Rebels (November 1, 2016): http://corporate-rebels.com/uktv.
5. Coert Visser, "Interview With Carol Dweck," The Progress-Focused Approach (February 28, 2007): http:// interviewscoertvisser.blogspot.com/2007/11/interview-with-carol -dweck_4897.html.
6. Janet Rae-Dupree, "If You're Open to Growth, You Tend to Grow," *New York Times* (July 6, 2008): www.nytimes .com/2008/07/06/business/06unbox.html.
7. Francesca Gino and Bradley Staats, "Why Organizations Don't Learn," *Harvard Business Review* (November 2015): https://hbr .org/2015/11/why-organizations-dont-learn.
8. Economist, "What Satya Nadella Did at Microsoft," *Economist* (March 16, 2017): www.economist.com/news /business/21718916-worlds-biggest-software-firm-has -transformed-its-culture-better-getting-cloud?.
9. John Baldoni, *12 Steps to Power Presence: How to Assert Your Authority to Lead* (New York: AMACON, 2010, p. 2-3).

10. Geary A. Rummler and Alan P. Brache, *Improving Performance: How to Manage the White Space in the Organization Chart* (San Francisco: Jossey-Bass, 1995).

11. Microsoft and Poptech, "The Changing World of Work: The Responsive Organization," Microsoft video, 5:25. Accessed April 11, 2017. http://news.microsoft.com/envisioning/part-five.html.

Chapter 3

1. Joost Minnaar and Pim de Morree, "FAVI (Part 1): How Zobrist Broke Down FAVI'S Command-and-Control Structures," Corporate Rebels (January 4, 2017): http://corporate-rebels.com /zobrist.

2. Ibid.

3. Liz Ryan, "Command-and-Control Management Is for Dinosaurs," *Forbes* (February 26, 2016): www.forbes.com/sites /lizryan/2016/02/26/command-and-control-management-is-for -dinosaurs/#3c6df12d24ed.

4. Chuck Blakeman, "At Nearsoft, No Managers and Complete Freedom to Create Responsibility, Not Anarchy," *Inc.* (November 17, 2015): www.inc.com/chuck-blakeman/at-nearsoft-no -managers-and-complete-freedom-create-responsibility-not -anarchy.html.

5. Joost Minnaar and Pim de Morree, "How Nearsoft Created Its Success? By Letting Go of Most of the Rules!" Corporate Rebels (November 10, 2016): http://corporate-rebels.com/nearsoft.

6. Ibid.

7. WorldBlu, *Freedom at Work: Growth & Resilience* (WorldBlu 2015): http://cdn2.hubspot.net/hubfs/621498 /Offers/WorldBlu_Freedom-at-Work_Growth--Resilience .pdf?submissionGuid=3ce006da-12de-4342-aef9-85a2f4bcd8e9.

8. Ibid.

9. Ibid.

10. Microsoft and Poptech, "The Changing World of Work: Leadership in Transition," Microsoft video, 6:54. Accessed April 11, 2017. http://news.microsoft.com/envisioning/part-five.html.

11. Joost Minnaar and Pim de Morree, "How to Radically Create a Happy Company From Scratch," Corporate Rebels (June 13, 2016): http://corporate-rebels.com/rene-van-loon.
12. Ibid.
13. Aimee Groth, "Internal Memo: Zappos Is Offering Severance to Employees Who Aren't All in With Holacracy," Quartz (March 26, 2015): https://qz.com/370616/internal-memo-zappos-is-offering-severance-to-employees-who-arent-all-in-with-holacracy.
14. Paul Solman, "Zappos Is a Weird Company—and It's Happy That Way," PBS NewsHour (March 2, 2017): www.pbs.org/newshour/bb/zappos-weird-company-happy-way.
15. Raj Aggarwal and Betty J. Simkins, "Open-Book Management—Optimizing Human Capital," Business Horizons 44 (May 2001): 5–13.
16. Jack Stack and Bo Burlingham, The Great Game of Business, Expanded and Updated: The Only Sensible Way to Run a Company (New York: Crown Business, 2013).
17. Ari Weinzweig, "Why Open Book Management Is an Excellent Way to Run a Business!" Zing Train, www.zingtrain.com/content/why-open-book-management-excellent-way-run-business.
18. Ibid.
19. James Pomeroy, "Rise of the Digital Natives: The Tech-Savvy Generation Is Changing the World's Economic Assumptions," HSBC Insights (September 12, 2016): www.gbm.hsbc.com/insights/economics/rise-of-the-digital-natives.
20. Pau Garcia Fuster, "Les millors empreses on treballar," Via Empresa (January 26, 2015): www.viaempresa.cat/ca/notices/2015/01/les-millors-empreses-on-treballar-10402.php.
21. Joost Minnaar and Pim de Morree, "Practical Happiness Tips From Our Bucket List Visit to Spain," Corporate Rebels (April 25, 2016): http://corporate-rebels.com/Blog/practical-happiness-tips-spain.
22. Alton Chua, review of Cultivating Communities of Practice, by Etienne Wenger, Richard McDermott, and William Snyder, Journal of Knowledge Management Practice (October 2002).

Chapter 4

1. The Kirkpatrick model defines four levels of evaluation: Level 1 (Reaction), Level 2 (Learning), Level 3 (Behavior), and Level 4 (Results). James D. and Wendy Kayser Kirkpatrick, *Kirkpatrick's Four Levels of Evaluation* (Alexandria, VA: ATD Press, 2016).
2. Association for Talent Development (ATD), *Building a Culture of Learning: The Foundation of a Successful Organization* (Alexandria, VA: ATD Press, 2016).
3. Hermann Ebbinghaus, *Memory: A Contribution to Experimental Psychology,* translated by Henry A. Ruger and Clara E. Bussenius (New York: Teachers College, Columbia University, 1913). http://psychclassics.yorku.ca/Ebbinghaus/index.htm.
4. Andrew Jefferson and Roy Pollock. "70:20:10: Where Is the Evidence?" ATD Science of Learning Blog (July 8, 2014): www.td.org/Publications/Blogs/Science-of-Learning-Blog/2014/07/70-20-10-Where-Is-the-Evidence.
5. David Grebow, "At the Water Cooler of Learnng," Marcia Conner blog (January 26, 2003): http://marciaconner.com/blog/water-cooler-learning.

Chapter 5

1. Malcolm Knowles, *Self-Directed Learning: A Guide for Learners and Teachers* (New York: Cambridge Books, 1975).
2. Daniel Pink, "The Puzzle of Motivation," TED video, 18:36. July 2009. www.ted.com/talks/dan_pink_on_motivation/transcript?language=en.
3. Josh Bersin, "Why Companies Fail To Engage Today's Workforce: The Overwhelmed Employee," *Forbes* (March 15, 2014): www.forbes.com/sites/joshbersin/2014/03/15/why-companies-fail-to-engage-todays-workforce-the-overwhelmed-employee/#7da0f0d44726.
4. Harold Jarche, "The Future of the Training Department," Poll Everywhere (October 21, 2009): http://jarche.com/2009/10/the-future-of-the-training-department-2.

5. Fred Schmalz, "Former Walmart.com CEO Explains How to Nurture Star Employees." Yahoo! Finance (October 23, 2016): www.yahoo.com/news/former-walmart-com-ceo-explains-how-to -nurture-star-employees-142608823.html.

6. Daniel Pink, *A Whole New Mind: Why Right-Brainers Will Rule the Future* (New York: Penguin Group, 2006).

7. World Economic Forum, "The Future of Jobs," World Economic Forum (January 2016): www3.weforum.org/docs/WEF_Future _of_Jobs.pdf.

8. Etienne Wenger, *Communities of Practice: Learning, Meaning, and Identity* (Cambridge: Cambridge University Press, 1998).

9. Alton Chua, review of Cultivating Communities of Practice. (Chapter 3, n. 20).

10. Deborah Halber,"Why We Learn More From Our Successes Than Our Failures," MIT News (July 29, 2009): http://news.mit .edu/2009/successes-0729.

11. Shellye Archambeau, "What Is Your Company's Cost of Poor Quality?" Quality Digest (August 23, 2004): www.qualitydigest .com/inside/quality-insider-article/what-your-companyrsquos-cost -poor-quality.html.

Chapter 6

1. "Watch Dov Seidman at the 2016 Fortune-Time Global Forum," YouTube video, 1:05, posted by *Fortune Magazine,* December 2, 2016, www.youtube.com/watch?v=B2ZqEBLk1-8.

2. Ibid.

3. Worldblu, "10 Principles of Organizational Democracy," Worldblu (Accessed April 15, 2017): https://worldblu.com/democratic -design/principles.php.

4. John Baldoni, *The Leader's Pocket Guide: 101 Indispensable Tools, Tips, and Techniques for Any Situation* (New York: AMACOM, 2013).

5. Ibid.

6. Denene Brox, "14 Companies With Incredible Employee Perks," Salary.com (Accessed April 17, 2017). www.salary.com/14 -companies-with-incredible-employee-perks.

7. Joost Minnaar and Pim de Morree, "These 3 Practical Changes Boosted the Success and Happiness at UKTV," Corporate Rebels (November 1, 2016): http://corporate-rebels.com/uktv.

8. Ibid.

9. Steelcase, "Driving the Wellbeing of People: Why Smart + Connected Spaces Improve the Experiences People Have at Work," Steelcase (October 24, 2016): www.steelcase.com/insights/articles /driving-wellbeing-people.

10. Steelcase, "The Resilient Workplace," Steelcase (Accessed May 10, 2017): www.steelcase.com/eu-en/spaces inspiration/resilient -workplace.

11. Richard Sheridan, *Joy, Inc.: How We Built a Workplace People Love* (New York: Portfolio, 2015).

Chapter 7

1. Josh Davis and Kenny Davis, "Two Simple Steps to Sell Anybody on Your Vision," Fast Company (February 15, 2017): www .fastcompany.com/3068205/how-to-be-a-success-at-everything /two-simple-steps-to-sell-anybody-on-your-vision.

2. Ibid.

3. Ibid.

4. Gary L. Neilson and Jaime Estupiñán, "The 10 Principles of Organizational DNA," *strategy + business* (October 27, 2014): www.strategy-business.com/blog/The-10-Principles-of -Organizational-DNA?gko=c5b42.

5. Stephen J. Gill and Sean P. Murray, *Getting More From Your Investment in Training: The 5As Framework* (Seattle: RealTime Performance, 2009).

6. Edgar H. Schein, *Organizational Culture and Leadership*, 4th Edition (San Francisco: Jossey-Bass, 2010).

7. David A. Garvin, Amy C. Edmondson, and Francesca Gino, "Is Yours a Learning Organization?" *Harvard Business Review* (March 2008): https://hbr.org/2008/03/is-yours-a-learning-organization.
8. James D. Stilwell, "How to Use Feedback From Employee Surveys to Change Organizations," The Performance Improvement Blog (July 23, 2010): http://stephenjgill.typepad.com/performance _improvement_b/2010/07/how-to-use-feedback-from-employee -surveys-to-change-organizations.html.

Chapter 8

1. Edgar H. Schein, "Innovative Cultures and Adaptive Organizations," in *Creating a Learning Culture: Strategy, Technology, and Practice* (New York: Cambridge University Press, 2004), 123-151.
2. Marcia L. Conner and James G. Clawson, *Creating a Learning Culture: Strategy, Technology, and Practice* (Cambridge: Cambridge University Press, 2004).
3. R. Buckminster Fuller, *Critical Path* (New York: St. Martin's Press, 1981).
4. Ricardo Semler, "How to Run a Company With (Almost) No Rules," TED video, 21:42. October 2014. www.ted.com/talks /ricardo_semler_radical_wisdom_for_a_company_a_school_a _life/transcript?language=en.
5. Ibid.
6. Michael Collins, "The Kind of Training We Need in Manufacturing," *IndustryWeek* (April 30, 2015): www .industryweek.com/recruiting-retention/kind-training-we-need -manufacturing.
7. Ibid.

Afterword

1. Studs Terkel, *Working: People Talk About What They Do All Day and How They Feel About What They Do* (New York: The New Press, 1972).

2. National Public Radio (NPR), "'Working' Then and Now: 'I Didn't Plan to Be a Union Guy,'" NPR (September 29, 2016): www.npr.org/templates/transcript/transcript .php?storyId=495916035.

3. Amy X. Wang, "Why Everyone Is So Mad: 99% of Post-Recession Jobs Went to Those Who Went to College," Quartz (July 1, 2016): http://qz.com/721854/why-everyone-is-so-mad-99-of-post -recession-jobs-went-to-those-who-went-to-college.

4. Ibid.

5. JP Gownder, "Robots Won't Steal All the Jobs—But They'll Transform the Way We Work," JP Gownder's Blog, Forrester (August 24, 2015): http://blogs.forrester.com/jp_gownder/15-08 -24-robots_wont_steal_all_the_jobs_but_theyll_transform_the _way_we_work.

6. Ibid.

7. Anita Balakrishnan, "Bezos Shareholder Letter: Don't Let the World Push You Into Becoming a 'Day 2' Company," CNBC (April 12, 2017): www.cnbc.com/2017/04/12/amazon-jeff-bezos -2017-shareholder-letter.html.

ACKNOWLEDGMENTS

The words in this book are like an iceberg: What you read is just the tip of all the thinking, discussing, reading, researching, reviewing, arguing, refining, and rewriting that went into it. We did the work of writing the words, and get to put our names on the cover. Yet that's only part of the story.

There are many people who inspired us, made us sit up and take notice, forced us to get behind our assumptions, and provided us with enough confirmation to make us believe the ideas in this book are valid.

Many thanks to the following people:

All the friends who drank with us, fed us, held our hands, watched us vent, and more than anything, listened to us as we talked through the ideas, especially Jacques Seronde, Howard Berens, Danie Watson, Ana Santos, Virginia Sargent, James Stilwell, Theo Jolosky, Bernard Donkerbrook, Jesse Bernstein, Ralph Jacobson, Megan Torrance, and Louis M. Callaway Jr.

Ryan Changcoco from ATD, who "got it" from the first time we started talking about the book, and read the initial draft nonstop on a trip from Washington, D.C., to New York. Susan Leigh Fry, who understands how ideas turn into words and the words then get to the point. And our ATD editors, Jonathan Harlow and Caroline Coppel, who between them made the words you're reading more readable. We never had a problem with their edits because they recognized the difference between good and really good writing.

Joost Minnaar and Pim de Morree, known as the "Corporate Rebels," for their amazing work finding and learning from the companies on their "Bucket List." Many of those companies are the leading edge of the wave of organizations discovering every day what it means to manage minds.

A long list of people stretching back well into our past from whom we took inspiration. The people whose ideas we draw on over and over include Thomas L. Friedman, Josh Bersin, Mark Powell, Jonathan Gifford, Daniel Pink, Rachel Botsman, Brian Robertson, Don Tapscott, Dov Seidman, Jim Whitehurst, Linda Hill, Jane Hart, Katy Tynan, Marcia L. Conner, Robert O. Brinkerhoff, Richard Sheridan, Ari Weinzweig, Chris Argyris, Edgar Schein, David Garvin, Amy Edmondson, Peter Senge, John Baldoni, Maggie Bayless, Harold Jarche, Robert Pasick, Carol Dweck, Sean P. Murray, and Wally Bock.

All the people who work in the companies we mention, who are learning what it means to work in an organization that truly cares about learning. They helped us see how success in the new economy needs to be built on a different way of managing and learning we call managing minds.

And you, our readers, who we imagine are reading this book trying to learn what it would be like to work in an organization that is open and honest, where trust is the norm, and communication and collaboration are the way business gets done. An organization that fully recognizes and respects who you are, how you think, and what you have to say and can do.

Our hope is that someday you go to work feeling completely fearless and empowered to give all you are and will be, for yourself and others.

ABOUT THE AUTHORS

 **David Grebow** is CEO of KnowledgeStar, and an author, popular speaker, and workshop leader. KnowledgeStar is a consulting firm founded in 2006 to provide insight about the intersection of digital technology and education. Its clients include Fortune 500 corporations, startups, NGOs, and leading analyst firms Bersin & Associates and the Brandon Hall Group. KnowledgeStar is currently involved in launching an interactive performance support system that automatically delivers just-in-time knowledge to people working in manufacturing environments.

For 25 years prior to starting KnowledgeStar, David held senior development and management positions with leading technology and education companies, including IBM, where he co-founded the Institute for Advanced Learning; PeopleSoft; Cisco; and McGraw-Hill. David is a co-author of *Creating a Learning Culture* with Marcia Conner and James Clawson and served on the editorial review board for Information Age Publishing, working to produce a series of books on technology and learning. David also writes The KnowledgeStar Blog, one of the most widely read blogs on learning and technology. He has authored numerous research papers and articles for publications in the corporate education industry. He lives in San Francisco, and can be reached at david@mind-satwork.co.

Stephen J. Gill is the co-owner of www
.learningtobegreat.com, a resource for creating
and sustaining a learning culture in organizations, and owner and principal of Stephen J. Gill
Consulting. Steve's expertise is in creating learning cultures in organizations and measuring the
impact of learning and performance improvement solutions. He has done this work for more
than 25 years, since leaving the faculty of the
University of Michigan School of Education. He has written extensively
about these topics.

Steve's most recent books are *Getting More From Your Investment
in Training: The 5As Framework*, published by RealTime Performance
in 2009; *Developing a Learning Culture in Nonprofit Organizations*,
published by Sage Publications in 2010; and *Communication in High
Performance Organizations: Principles and Best Practices*, published
as a Kindle e-book in 2011. Steve also posts regularly on the Performance Improvement Blog. He served 12 years as an elected trustee of
Washtenaw Community College. He lives in Ann Arbor, Michigan,
and can be reached at steve@mindsatwork.co.

INDEX

acting fearlessly, 30–31
feedback, 63, 106
Fenton, Traci, 31
fixed mindset, 19–20
the forgetting curve, 48, 54
Foster, Richard, 1
freedom, personal, 31
future workplaces
    accessibility of information,
        106
    feedback, 106
    imagining, 105–107
    project evaluations and reviews,
        107
    strategic planning, 107

G

Gery, Gloria, 50
Geus, Arie de, 6
Gilmartin, Ray, 2
goals
    setting company goals from
        personal goals, 37
golf example of the pivot point, 56
Google example of continuous
    learning, 60
growth mindset, 19–22, 61–62, 90

H

Harvard Business School survey on
    corporate culture, 101–102
holacracy
    about, 34
    Zappos example, 34
    Hsieh, Tony, 34
human capital, vii

I

incentives and recognition, 40, 63,
    91. See also rewards, extrinsic
    and intrinsic
independent learning, 12

information accessibility, 106
innovators, 87–88
instructor-led training (ILT), 7–9
intelligence
    emotional intelligence (EQ), 68
    IQ, 68
interactive learning, 12
Internet
    collective brainpower of the, 16
    and competition, 16–17

J

Jarche, Harold, 64
John example of e-learning
    systems, 52–54

K

Kavanaugh, Jeff, 5
knowledge
    four types, xiv, 38–39
    mind meld concept, 36
    sharing, 14–16, 40, 70, 90–91
knowledge workers, xii–xiv
Knowles, Malcolm, 60–61
Kodak, 2–3

L

lathe compliance check example of
    performance support, 50–51
"leadership presence," 23–24, 113
*The Leader's Pocket Guide: 101
    Indispensable Tools, Tips, and
    Techniques* (Baldoni), 80
learning. *See also* education
    5 As for "managing minds,"
        95–100
    accountability for the learning
        process, 99–100
    aligning learning and results on
        the job, 95–96
    alliance between management
        and the learners, 97–98

"The Rise of the Digital Natives"
(essay), 36
risks
of moving towards a "managing
minds" model, 108–109
taking risks on the job, 20, 30,
71–72, 91
robotics
Studs Terkel/Gary Bryner
interview, 115–117
Zume Pizza example, 3–4

S

Saint-Exupéry, Antoine de, 105
Schein, Edgar Henry, 100–101,
108
scientific management theory, xii
Seidman, Dov, 78
self-directed learning
active participation, 66
autonomy, mastery, and
purpose, 61
communication skills, 66
creating an environment for,
61, 90
creativity, 67
critical thinking skills, 65
curating information, 64–65
defined, 60–61
emotional intelligence (EI), 68
examples of results from
effective, 63–64
learner's role, 62
management's role, 61–64
performance feedback, 63
self-reflection, 67
Semco example of "managing
minds" successfully, 110–112
Semler, Ricardo, 110–112
shared consciousness
principles of, 31–33

pyramid and ball example,
32–33
Van Loon Elektrotechniek
example, 33
sharing knowledge
in a community of learners and
practice, 70
encouraging, 40, 90–91
NGO example of hoarding
learning and training,
14–15
shifting from a "managing
hands" to a "managing minds"
environment
corporate culture, 89–95,
100–103
innovators, 87–88
investment required, 107–108
making the case, 87–88
protectors, 87–88
values, 92–95
social learning, 12–13, 69–70
speed of change, 25, 59–60,
107–108
Spicer, André, 13
Stanford University example of
outdated learning, 5
Star Trek (TV show), 36
Steelcase, 86
Stephenson, Randall, xvii
Stilwell, Jim, 102
strategic planning, 107
The Stupidity Paradox (Spicer and
Alvesson), 13

T

the 21st-century corporation
critical thinking skills, 65
curation of information, 64–65
demise of companies that did
not evolve, 2–3